# SINAN

ARCHITECT OF SÜLEYMAN

THE MAGNIFICENT

AND THE

OTTOMAN GOLDEN AGE

JOHN FREELY

AUGUSTO ROMANO BURELLI

PHOTOGRAPHS BY ARA GULER

THAMES AND HUDSON

THE SIGNATURE OF SINAN
(PAGE 1), ENGRAVED ON THE BRIDGE OF BÜYÜK ÇEKMECE,
ERECTED IN 1567. IT READS "WORK OF YUSUF, SON OF
ABDULLAH". SINAN'S FULL NAME WAS SINANÜDDIN YUSUF; HIS
PATRONYMIC INDICATES THAT HIS ANCESTORS WERE NOT
MUSLIM. PAGE 2: THE SEMSI PASHA CAMII (THE MOSQUE OF
SEMSI PASHA, COURT POET), BUILT IN 1580, REFLECTED IN THE
WATERS OF THE BOSPHORUS. PAGES 6-7 AND 8-9: THE
SÜLEYMANIYE IS A COMPLEX ENSEMBLE OF DOMES
AND SEMIDOMES INSCRIBED IN A PYRAMID, ANCHORED BY
TALL, SLENDER MINARETS.

EDITORIAL COORDINATOR
MARIE AMÉLIE BERI

DESIGNER
PATRICK LÉBÉDEFF

EDITOR
BARBARA ROSEN

FIRST PUBLISHED IN GREAT BRITAIN IN 1992
BY THAMES AND HUDSON LTD, LONDON
FIRST PUBLISHED IN THE UNITED STATES OF AMERICA
IN 1992 BY THAMES AND HUDSON INC.,
500 FIFTH AVENUE, NEW YORK, NEW YORK 10110

**ARCHITECT AND ENGINEER**
— 11 —

**A TESTAMENT IN STONE**
— 51 —

**SPACE AND LIGHT**
— 71 —

**STATICS AND STYLE**
— 121 —

پیشوای زمرهٔ انبیا مقتدای زمرهٔ اصفیا مصطفی نك صلی الله علیه وسلم محمد مصطفی

معجزات کثیرهٔ البرکانی ودر ترتابندهک که ابو بکر و عمر و عثمان و علی رضوان الله تعالی

علیهم اجمعین انلرك وجمعی اولیالرك ارواح فلاح اشباحلری مواق

سلطان بن سلطان یاوز ...

وه یار بک و کوک ...

Architecture is
the most difficult
of professions, and he
who would practise
it must, above all
things, be pious.
*SINAN*

S tretching along both shores of the Bosphorus, the strait that separates Europe and Asia between the Black Sea and the Sea of Marmara in the north-western corner of Turkey, Istanbul is the only city in the world that stands astride two continents. The city is further divided by the Golden Horn, the scimitar-shaped stream that enters the strait on its European side just before the Bosphorus flows into the Marmara. The oldest section of the city, Stamboul, known to the Greeks as Constantinople and to the ancients as Byzantium, is on the right bank of the Golden Horn. On the left bank near the Bosphorus is the port quarter of Galata, with the more modern neighbourhoods stretching out along the hills to the north. Across the strait in Asia are Üsküdar and Kadíköy, which in antiquity were known as Chrysopolis and Chalcedon, respectively. The walls of the old city enclose seven hills, six rising from the ridge above the Golden Horn and the seventh standing all by itself to the south-west near the Marmara. The first of these hills rises above Saray Burnu, or Palace Point, the acropolis where the ancient Greek city of Byzantium was founded circa 660 BC at the confluence of the Bosphorus and the Golden Horn. The two most splendid of these landmarks are Haghia Sophia and the Süleymaniye, each the supreme architectural achievement of the world empires that had their capitals here at the confluence of the Bosphorus and the Golden Horn, the Byzantines from 330-1453 and the Ottomans from 1453-1923. These two imperial monuments, erected more than a thousand years apart in time, are separated by only a mile in Istanbul, both of them visible in one view of the skyline of the imperial city above the Golden Horn.

## THE OSMANLÍ DYNASTY

The sultans who ruled the Ottoman Empire were descendants of Osman Gazi. In 1326, Osman's son Orhan Gazi, the first Osmanlí sultan, captured the Bithynian city of Bursa (the Greek Prusa), making it the first capital of the Ottoman realm. The Osmanlí expanded rapidly from that point on, crossing the Dardanelles in the mid-fourteenth century and in 1363 capturing the Thracian city of Edirne (Adrianople), shifting their capital there as a base for their almost annual campaigns into the Balkans, while at the same time expanding eastward into Anatolia. The Osmanlí were briefly checked in 1402, when Tamerlane defeated Sultan Beyazit at the battle of Ankara, leading to an interregnum that lasted for more than a decade, until Mehmet I became sole ruler

S ÜLEYMAN'S MONOGRAM (PAGE 10), ON A LETTER ADDRESSED TO FRANÇOIS I OF FRANCE IN 1536. OPPOSITE: A COPY OF A LOST PORTRAIT OF SÜLEYMAN, FROM SCHLOSS AMBRASS IN AUSTRIA. AN ADMIRING, APPREHENSIVE EUROPE WAS EAGER TO PROCURE PORTRAITS OF SULTAN SÜLEYMAN. TITIAN PAINTED FOUR LIKENESSES – ALTHOUGH HE NEVER MET SÜLEYMAN IN THE FLESH. HE PROBABLY USED DRAWINGS FROM THE ORIENT AS A MODEL FOR THE PORTRAITS.

in 1413 and began to recapture the lost dominions of the Empire. By the middle of the fifteenth century, the Ottoman Empire included most of south-eastern Europe and western Asia Minor, with the Byzantine Empire reduced to little more than Constantinople and its environs. The Byzantine Empire came to an end in 1453, when Constantinople fell to Mehmet II, who thereafter was known to the Turks as Fatih, or the Conqueror. Fatih soon shifted his capital to Constantinople, which the Turks called Istanbul, a corruption of the Greek "stin poli," meaning "in the city" or "to the city". During the remaining years of his reign (1451-81), Fatih made additional conquests in southern Europe and Anatolia, at the same time rebuilding Istanbul to suit its role as the capital of a powerful Muslim empire. Fatih was succeeded by Beyazit II (1481-1512), who consolidated the resources of the empire and developed its trade and commerce. He was succeeded by Selim I (1512-20), who increased the Ottoman dominions in Asia and captured Cairo in 1517, after which the Ottoman rulers assumed the titular leadership of Islam, adding the title of Caliph to that of Sultan.

The Osmanlí Turks reached the pinnacle of their power under Süleyman the Magnificent, who ruled from 1520-66, the longest reign in the history of the Ottoman Empire. Süleyman, known to the Turks as Kanuni, or the Lawgiver, personally led his army in a dozen victorious campaigns, extending the borders of his empire to include Asia Minor, western Persia, the Middle East, Egypt, the North African shore, Greece and the Aegean Islands, and the Balkans as far as Hungary, where he died at Sziget in 1566, on his last expedition. During Süleyman's reign the imperial city at the confluence of the Bosphorus and the Golden Horn was once again the resplendent capital of a world empire, a thousand years after the golden age of Byzantium under Justinian.

Most of the principal edifices of the Ottoman Empire, and many of the lesser ones too, were designed and built by Mimar (the Architect) Sinan, who was Chief Imperial Architect under Süleyman and his two immediate successors, Selim II (1566-74) and Murat III (1574-95). Sinan is credited with a total of 477 buildings, of which 336 were erected in Istanbul and its environs. The remaining 141 were scattered around the former provinces of the Ottoman Empire, including present-day Turkey, Greece, Bulgaria and Hungary, as well as Mecca, Medina, Jerusalem, Damascus, Aleppo, Basra and Baghdad. His structures include large mosques, small mosques (*mescit*), tombs (*türbe*), theological schools (*medrese*), schools for reading the Koran (*dar-ül kura*), primary schools (*mektep*), dervish monasteries (*tekke*), hospitals (*dar-üs-sifa*), public kitchens (*imaret*), inns for travelers (caravanserais), palaces (*saray* or *kasír*), pavilions (*kösk*), warehouses (*han*), public baths (*hamam*), bridges (*köprü*), and aqueducts (*sukemeri*). Most of Sinan's structures are still standing and in good repair after more than three centuries of constant use, reminding one of the tremendous vitality and vast extent of the Ottoman Empire under Süleyman and his immediate successors.

## JANISSARY AND ARCHITECT

Sinan was born in the Anatolian province of Karamania in the last decade of the fifteenth century, probably around 1497 (though some place his birth as early as 1491). His parents were Christians, probably Armenian or Greek. In his youth he was caught up in the *devsirme*, the annual levy of Christian youths who were enrolled in the Sultan's service. As was customary, he became a Muslim, taking the name Sinan, and was sent as a cadet to one of the palace schools in Istanbul, learning carpentry and other building trades. He was assigned to the Janissaries, the elite corps of the Ottoman Army, as a military engineer. During the next two decades he served in seven of Süleyman's victorious campaigns: Belgrade (1521), Rhodes (1522), Mohacs (1526), Germany (1529), the Two Iraqs (Baghdad and Basra, 1534), Corfu and Apulia (1537), and Moldavia (1538). These campaigns gave Sinan the opportunity to travel widely in Asia and Europe, where he would have become acquainted with Islamic and Christian architecture, as well as the earlier Turkish and Byzantine architecture of Istanbul and the other cities of Turkey. During these expeditions he acquired experience in erecting and repairing bridges, fortresses and other structures. Sinan's earliest known realisation is the bridge built for Çoban Mustafa Pasha in 1528-29 at Svilengrad in Bulgaria. His first mosque is the little Üç Bas Mescit in Istanbul, erected in 1530-31. In 1533-34 Sinan built a mosque for Süleyman in Van, in far eastern Anatolia, and a bridge for the sultan at Dil Iskelesi in Kocaeli Province. That same year he built two *mescit* in Istanbul, and within the two following years he erected two domed mosques in the provinces, one for Hadím (the Eunuch) Ali Pasha in Diyarbakir and the other for Hüsrev Pasha in Aleppo. This burst of activity marked Sinan's emergence as a professional architect. After his last campaign in Moldavia in 1538, as a Janissary, Sinan was appointed by Süleyman as *Mimarbasí*, Chief of the Imperial Architects. Sinan was to hold this post for half a

SINAN MIGHT NEVER HAVE REALISED HIS GREATEST ACCOMPLISHMENTS IF NOT FOR THE MONUMENTAL PRESENCE OF HAGHIA SOPHIA. JUSTINIAN'S GREAT BASILICA, ERECTED IN THE SIXTH CENTURY IN CONSTANTINOPLE, PROVIDED BOTH A MODEL AND A CHALLENGE THROUGHOUT SINAN'S LONG CAREER.. FOLLOWING PAGES: DETAIL OF A VIEW OF ISTANBUL FROM THE GOLDEN HORN, WITH HAGHIA SOPHIA TO THE LEFT, PAINTED IN 1557 BY THE DANISH ARTIST MELCHIOR LORICHS.

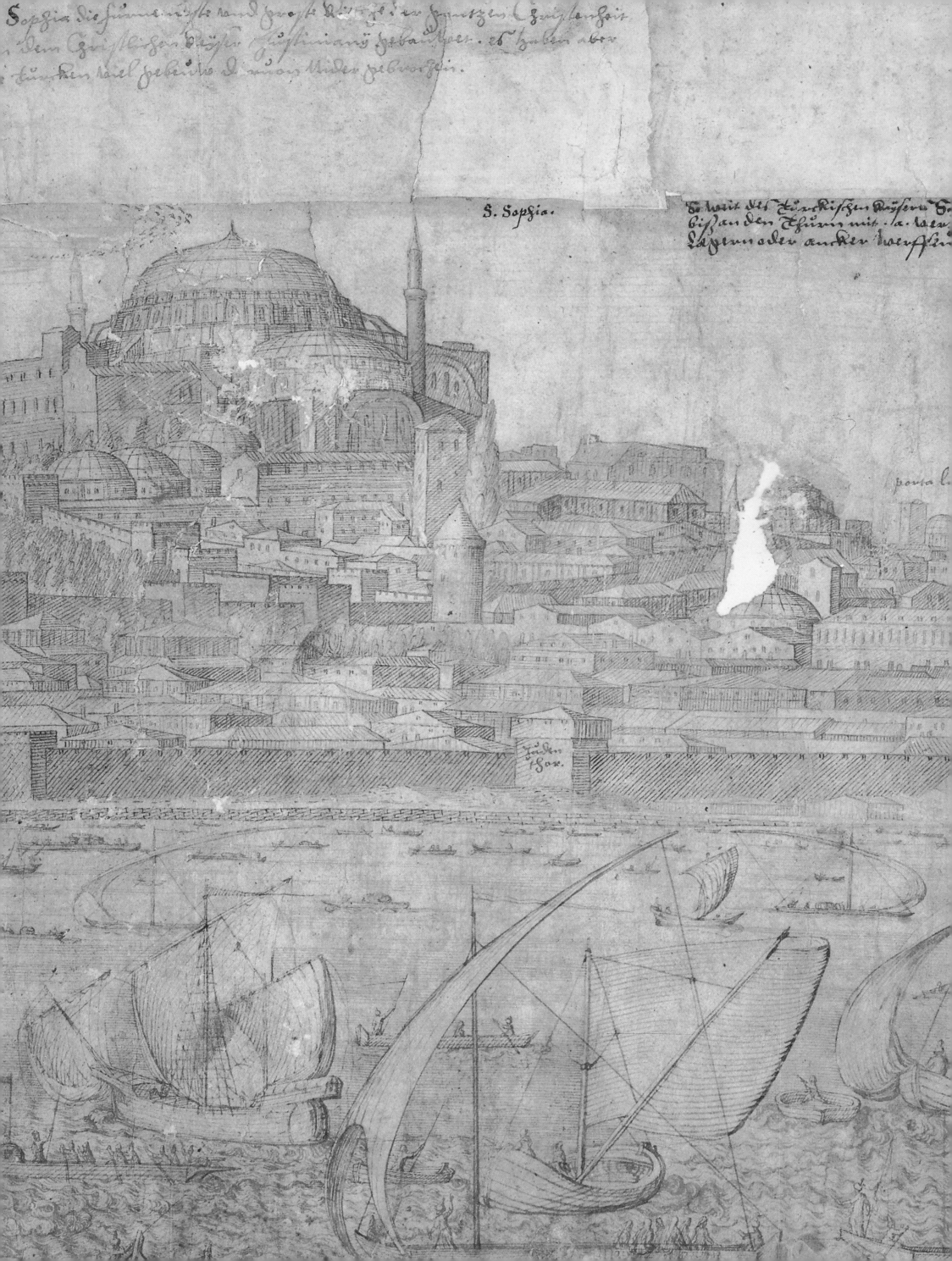

S. Sophia.

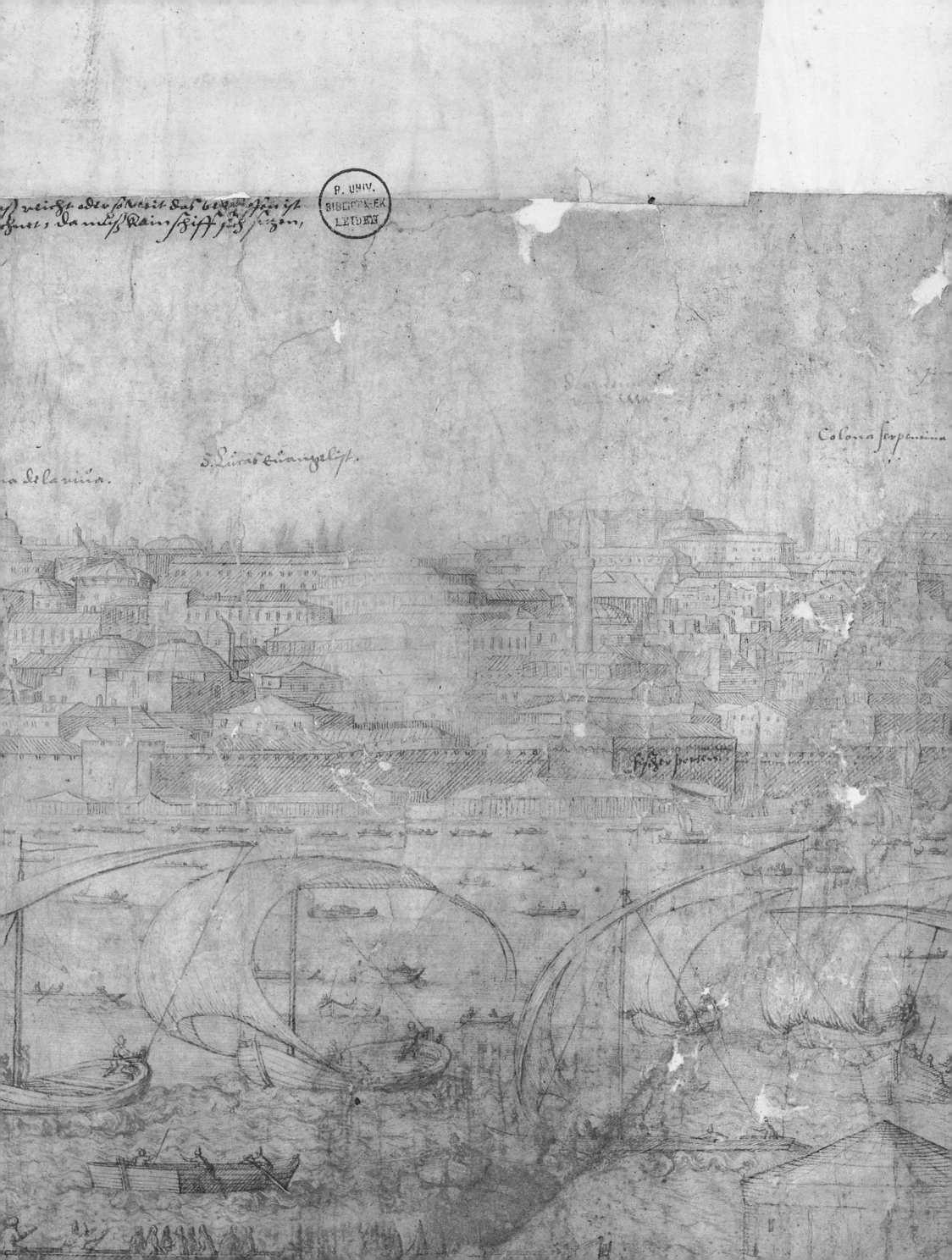

reicht oder schreit das beschwert ist
...daß... da... keine Schiff... zuzogen,

...a de la viña.

S. Lucas euangelist.

Colona serpentina

century, during which time he was the principal force in the development of classical Ottoman architecture, the style that adorned Istanbul and the other cities of the empire with most of their greatest Islamic buildings.

## CHIEF OF THE IMPERIAL ARCHITECTS

As chief architect, Sinan was responsible for all building projects initiated by the sultan and his grand vezir, the latter post being held at the time by Lutfi Pasha, who had recommended his appointment as *Mimarbasí*. Sinan's first task came from Süleyman himself, and that was to build a mosque complex for his wife, Haseki Hürrem, better known in the West as Roxelana. Haseki Hürrem Camii was completed in 1538, when Süleyman presented it to his wife as a surprise birthday present, but the other elements of the *külliye*, or complex, were not finished until 1539. The original mosque consisted of a small square room covered by a masonry dome on stalactited pendentives, preceded by a porch of five bays that overlapped the building at both ends. This arrangement was altered by an awkward rebuilding in 1612. The other buildings of the Haseki Hürrem *külliye* have survived in their original form and have been well restored in recent years; including the *medrese*, hospital, primary school and *imaret*. The *medrese* is of the usual type – a porticoed courtyard surrounded by the students' cells (*hücre*) and the lecture-hall (*dershane*) – but though of truly imperial size, it is singularly well-proportioned and excellent in detail. The hospital is a building of most unusual form, with its various rooms arrayed in an irregular fashion around an octagonal courtyard. The *imaret* is more regular, with five huge double-domed kitchens arranged around the three sides of a porticoed courtyard, with the entryway in the fourth side. The primary school is large and oddly shaped, built in two storeys with wide projecting eaves.

Haseki Hürrem Camii was evidently successful, for soon after its completion Sinan was given commissions to build two more imperial mosque complexes. The first of these was founded by the Princess Mihrimah, Süleyman's daughter, for whom Sinan erected a mosque on the Bosphorus at Üsküdar. The second was founded by Süleyman, who had Sinan build a mosque on the Third Hill in memory of his son Prince (Sehzade) Mehmet, who died of smallpox in 1543 at twenty-one. The edifice that Sinan erected for Mihrimah on the Bosphorus (he later built another one for her on the Sixth Hill) is known as Iskele Camii, the Mosque of the Landing-Place, because

THE ENTRANCE TO THE FORMER NARTHEX OF HAGHIA SOPHIA (OPPOSITE), NOW THE VESTIBULE OF THE MOSQUE. PAGE 20: THE NATURALISTIC MOTIFS THAT DECORATE THE MARBLE OF HAGHIA SOPHIA ARE IN KEEPING WITH THE MUSLIM AVERSION TO REPRESENTATIONS OF THE HUMAN FIGURE. LARGE MEDALLIONS BEAR THE NAMES OF ALLAH, THE PROPHET MOHAMMED AND THE FOUR CALIPHS (IN THIS CASE, OMAR).

it stands beside the ferry-station (*iskele*) at the seaside square of Üsküdar. It was completed in 1547-48. The exterior is very imposing, due to its dominant position high above the square and its great double porch, a curious projection from which covers a charming fountain. The interior is perhaps less satisfactory, because the central dome is supported by three instead of the usual two or four semidomes, which gives it a rather truncated appearance. The *külliye* also includes a *medrese*, which is a pretty building of the rectangular type and is now used as a clinic, as well as a primary school that currently serves as a children's library.

The mosque that Sinan erected for Süleyman – Sehzade Mehmet Camii – was built in 1543-49. It was his first imperial mosque complex on a truly monumental scale, and Sinan rose to the challenge. Though he later referred to Sehzade Camii as his "apprentice work", it was truly the work of an apprentice of genius. The mosque is preceded by a handsome *avlu*, or forecourt, surrounded with a porticoed courtyard, with a *sardirvan*, or ablutions fountain, in the centre. The two minarets, which rise from the western corners of the mosque, are considered the most beautiful in the city, with their elaborate geometric sculptures in low relief, their intricate traceries of the balconies (*serefe*), and the occasional terracotta inlay. A cluster of domes and semidomes, many with fretted cornices and bold ribbing, crowns the building in an arrangement of repetition and contrast that is nowhere surpassed. Sinan first adopted the expedient of placing colonnaded galleries along the entire length of the north and south façades to conceal the buttresses, an arrangement that he would later use with greater effect at the Süleymaniye. This is certainly one of the finest exteriors that Sinan created. The interior is vast and empty: almost alone among the imperial mosques, it has not a single column, nor are there any galleries. Sinan, wishing from the beginning to centralise his plan, adopted the expedient of extending the area not by two semidomes, as in Haghia Sophia, but by four. Although this is the most logical way of increasing the space and centralising the plan, the identical symmetry along both axes has a repetitive effect. Furthermore, the four great piers that support the dome are isolated in the midst of the vast space and their large size is unduly emphasised. The effect is of an austere simplicity.

Sinan was beginning to develop in his imperial mosque a new architectural concept, in which a vast prayer room of centralised plan, unobstructed by unnecessary and

Women generally did not pray in mosques, but the gynaeceum of Haghia Sophia (page 21), reserved for the empress, was a useful innovation that the Ottomans adapted for their mosques. Haghia Sophia was oriented toward Jerusalem; the Ottomans had only to make a slight adjustment in the axis, to orient the *mihrab* (opposite), the niche in the wall toward which worshippers pray, in the direction of Mecca.

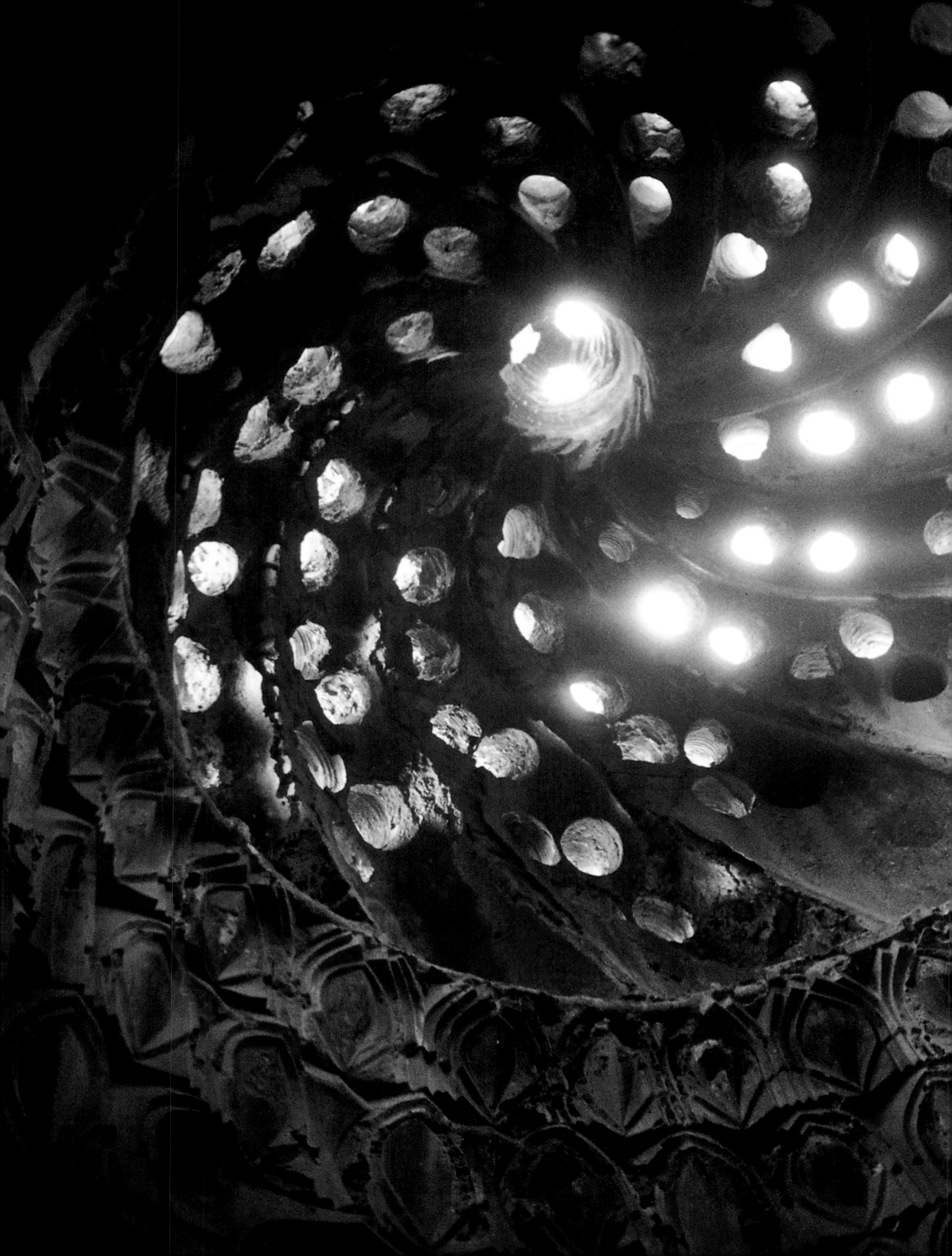

obstrusive columns or piers, is covered by a soaring dome. Haghia Sophia was always the archetype of the imperial Ottoman mosques of the classical period, though their plans in detail varied considerably from that of the great church.

Behind the mosque there is a walled graveyard garden with half-a-dozen tombs. The largest *türbe* in the centre of the garden is that of the Sehzade Mehmet himself. It is octagonal in form, the faces separated by slender engaged columns. The stonework is polychrome, with panels of verd antique inset here and there in the façades, while the window frames and arches are picked out in terracotta. The dome, which is double and carried on a fluted drum, is itself fluted. The small entrance porch has a fine pavement of opus sectile. It is a handsome building, in the ornately decorated style of the mosque exterior. The interior decoration surpasses that of any other *türbe* in Turkey in its tiles, woodwork, arabesque painting and stained-glass windows. Unfortunately, it is not open to the public, nor are the other fine tombs in the garden. The most notable of these is the *türbe* of the Grand Vezir Rüstem Pasha, husband of the Princess Mihrimah, built by Sinan in 1560-61. The other institutions of the Sehzade *külliye* stand along the north side of the mosque precincts and include a *medrese*, a *tabhane* (hospice), an *imaret* and a *mektep*, all of which have been well restored.

### THE SÜLEYMANIYE

The success of the Sehzade *külliye* demonstrated Sinan's genius, and the year after its completion Süleyman commissioned him to build the Süleymaniye, choosing a site on the summit of the Third Hill overlooking the Golden Horn. Sinan began building the Süleymaniye in 1550 and completed the mosque in 1557, but it took two more years before all the buildings of the *külliye* were finished. The mosque stands in the centre of a vast outer courtyard enclosed by a precinct wall, with most of the other buildings of the *külliye* arrayed around it on the surrounding streets. On the north side, where the land slopes sharply down to the Golden Horn, the courtyard is supported by an elaborate vaulted terrace, an extension of the outermost ridge of the Third Hill. The mosque is preceded by the usual *avlu*, a porticoed courtyard with columns of the richest porphyry, marble and granite. The western part of the court is flanked by a great pylon containing two storeys of chambers. The four minarets rise from the corners of the courtyard; each of the two taller ones beside the mosque has three *serefe*, the smaller

THE DOME OF THE IZNIK (NICAEA) HAMAM (PRECEDING PAGES), FROM WHICH LIGHT DELICATELY FILTERS DOWN. THE GRANDEUR OF HAGHIA SOPHIA SHOULD NOT ECLIPSE OTTOMAN ACHIEVEMENTS: NOT EVERYTHING ORIGINATED IN BYZANTIUM. THE SELÇUK TURKS, WHO CAME FROM CENTRAL ASIA ACROSS PERSIA AND MESOPOTAMIA, CREATED THE FIRST IDENTIFIABLY TURKISH ART IN ANATOLIA, OF WHICH THIS IS ONE EXAMPLE.

ones have two each. The great dome is flanked by semidomes, and on the north and south sides by arches whose tympanum walls are filled with windows. Internally, the dome is supported by four huge piers supported laterally by huge buttresses, which Sinan sought to make unobtrusive by a very ingenious plan. On the north and south, he incorporated the buttresses into the walls of the building, allowing them to project about equally within and without. He then proceeded to mask the projection by building galleries with arcades of columns between the buttresses. On the outside the gallery is double, with twice the number of columns in the upper storey as in the lower, while on the inside there is a single gallery. In both cases – particularly on the outside – the device is completely successful, and is indeed one of the features that give the exterior its interesting and beautiful distinction. On the east and west façades the buttresses are smaller, for there the weight of the dome is distributed by the semidomes. This led Sinan to place the eastern buttresses outside the building, where their moderate projection gives emphasis and variety to that façade. But on the west, in order to preserve the unity and grandeur of the western façade, he chose to place the buttresses within the building. Again he masked them with galleries, but in this case the device was inadequate. The great west portal, instead of being impressive, seems squeezed by the projection of the buttresses, which throw it into shadow, but also abut in an unpleasing way on the two small domes on which the western semidome reposes.

The interior of the mosque is 61 metres long and 70 metres wide, its central area surmounted by a great dome, 26.2 metres in diameter and with its crown 49.5 metres above the floor. The central area is extended along the main axis by semidomes to east and west and exedrae at the corners; on either side, there are five domed areas flanked by the galleries. The only separation between the central area and the side aisles are the four piers and the two pairs of porphyry monoliths that support the tympanum walls in triple arcades. Two other pairs of porphyry monoliths, to north and south of those between the piers, support the domes of the two middle spaces on either side, with the gallery arcades extending between them and the side buttresses. The general effect of the interior is of a severely simple grandeur. Only the east wall is enlivened by some touches of colour. Here the lovely stained-glass windows are by the glazier known as Sarhos (the Drunkard) Ibrahim. The tiles, used with great restraint, are among the earliest examples of the technique of the Iznik kilns introduced in the mid-sixteenth

THE MOSQUE OF ÇOBAN MUSTAFA PASHA, THE GOVERNOR OF EGYPT (FOLLOWING PAGES). FROM EGYPT CAME A TASTE FOR KUFIC CALLIGRAPHY AND MARBLE MOSAICS, BUT SUCH ORNAMENTS REMAINED THE EXCEPTION RATHER THAN THE RULE IN TURKEY. THIS MOSQUE WAS ERECTED IN 1524 IN GEBZE (TODAY A SUBURB OF ISTANBUL). IT APPEARS TO HAVE BEEN MISTAKENLY ATTRIBUTED TO SINAN, WHO WAS NAMED CHIEF IMPERIAL ARCHITECT IN 1538.

century: leaf and flower motifs in turquoise, deep blue and red on a pure white ground. The *mihrab* (the niche in the wall toward which worshippers face) and *mimber* (pulpit) in Proconessian marble are of great simplicity and distinction, as is the woodwork, inlaid with ivory and mother-of-pearl, of the doors, window shutters, and the Koran *kürsü*, or preacher's chair. Throughout the building the inscriptions are by the most famous of Ottoman calligraphers, Ahmet Karahisarí.

The tombs of Süleyman and Roxelana are in the graveyard garden behind the mosque. Süleyman's *türbe*, as is fitting, is the largest and grandest of Sinan's mausoleums. It was completed in 1566, the year Süleyman died while on campaign in Hungary. The *türbe* is octagonal in form, surrounded by a pretty porch on columns. Like Sinan's tombs at Sehzade Camii, Süleyman's *türbe* has a double dome, with the interior dome supported by columns, its inner surface still retaining its characteristic painting in wine-red, black and gold. The walls of the interior are covered with Iznik tiles, twice as many in this small room as in all the vastness of the mosque itself. Süleyman is buried beneath the large cenotaph in the centre of the room, his casket surmounted by the huge white turban that he wore in life. Arrayed around him are the cenotaphs of his daughter, the Princess Mihrimah, and two later sultans, Süleyman II (1687-91) and Ahmet II (1691-95). The *türbe* of Roxelana stands just to the east of Süleyman's tomb: her tomb is smaller, but its tile decoration is even finer. The cylindrical base of the dome, slightly recessed from the octagonal cornice of the building itself, is decorated with a long inscription forming a kind of sculpted frieze. For some reason this tomb is not included in the standard list of Sinan's works, but it is almost certainly his creation. The *türbe* is dated 1558, the year of Roxelana's death.

The other elements of the Süleymaniye *külliye* are arrayed around the inner courtyard and along the streets bordering the outer precinct wall. These include seven *medrese* of Islamic law, one of them serving as a preparatory school for the others; a *tip medrese* (medical college); a hospital, which included an insane asylum; an *imaret*; a caravanserai; a primary school; a *dar-ül hadis*, or school of religious tradition; a *dar-ül kura*; a public bath, and a street of shops. The revenues from the latter two institutions contributed to the upkeep of the rest of the *külliye*. The Süleymaniye is the second-largest *külliye* ever built in the Ottoman Empire, surpassed in size but not in grandeur by that of Mehmet II. But since the original Fatih Camii was destroyed in 1766, to be

LIGHT FALLS SOFTLY FROM OPENINGS IN THE DOME (OPPOSITE), ENHANCING THE MARBLE FLOOR-MOSAICS AND SHOWING HOW SINAN WISELY BUILT UPON PAST LESSONS LEARNED. THIS IS THE HAMAM BUILT ACROSS FROM HAGHIA SOPHIA IN 1556 FOR HASEKI HÜRREM (BETTER KNOWN IN THE WEST AS ROXELANA), SÜLEYMAN'S FAVOURITE WIFE.

replaced by an inferior edifice, the imperial mosque complex of Süleyman the Magnificent remains the greatest extant example of its type in Turkey.

## THE MOSQUES OF RÜSTEM PASHA AND MIHRIMAH

During the decade that Sinan worked on the Süleymaniye, he completed more than a score of other structures, including a mosque for Rüstem Pasha in Istanbul beside the Golden Horn (1562), another for the Princess Mihrimah (1562-65) on the summit of the Sixth Hill beside the Edirne Gate, and Süleyman's *türbe* (1566). The two mosques are the finest that Sinan built during the latter years of Süleyman's reign. Rüstem Pasha Camii stands in the market area just upstream from the Galata Bridge, which crosses the lower Golden Horn. The mosque is built on a high terrace over an interesting complex of vaulted shops and warehouses, the rent from which went to maintain the *külliye*. Interior flights of steps lead up from the corners of the platform to a spacious and beautiful courtyard, unique in the city. The plan of the mosque is an octagon inscribed in a rectangle. The dome is flanked by four small semidomes in the diagonal of the building. The arches of the dome spring from four octagonal pillars, two on the north and two on the south, and from piers projecting from the east and west walls. To the north and south there are galleries supported by pillars and by small marble columns between them. Rüstem Pasha Camii is renowned for the beautiful tiles that almost cover its walls, not only in the interior but also on the façade of the porch. Like all the very best Turkish tiles, those of Rüstem Pasha are from the kilns of Iznik at its peak, circa 1555-1620. The most characteristic element of the Iznik tiles of this period is the tomato-red or "Armenian bole" pigment, like drops of fresh blood in the vividness of its colour. These exquisite tiles, in a wide variety of floral and geometric designs, cover the walls, the columns, the *mihrab* and the *mimber*, making this one of the most striking mosque interiors in the city.

Mihrimah Sultan Camii dominates the Sixth Hill beside the Edirne Gate. The *külliye* includes, besides the mosque, a *medrese*, a *türbe*, a double *hamam* and a long row of shops in the substructure of the terrace on which it is built. From the exterior the mosque is strong and dominant, as befits its position at the highest point in the city. The square of the dome base with its multi-windowed tympana, identical on all sides, is given solidity and boldness by the four great weight-towers at the corners, prolongations of the piers

IN ADDITION TO HIS MOSQUES, SINAN ALSO CREATED MANY SUMPTUOUS PUBLIC EDIFICES. OPPOSITE AND ON THE FOLLOWING PAGES, TWO VIEWS OF THE CARAVANSERAI ERECTED FOR THE GRAND VEZIR RÜSTEM PASHA AROUND 1560 IN EDIRNE, THE EMPIRE'S SECOND CAPITAL. THIS INN FOR PASSING CARAVANS WAS SO WELL LAID OUT THAT TODAY IT STILL SERVES – IN ITS ORIGINAL FORM – AS A HOTEL.

that support the dome arches. Above this square rests the dome itself on a circular drum pierced by windows. The mosque is preceded by a great courtyard, around three sides of which are the porticoes and cells of the *medrese*, with an attractive *sadírvan* in the centre. The entrance to the mosque is under an imposing porch of seven domed bays supported by eight marble and granite columns. This porch was originally preceded by another portico, doubtless with a sloping wooden roof supported on twelve columns, traces of which may be seen on the ground. This double porch was a favourite device of Sinan's, which he used earlier at Mihrimah's other mosque at Üsküdar and again in many other places. The central area of the interior is square, covered by a great dome 20 metres in diameter and 37 metres high under the crown, resting on smooth pendentives. The tympana of all four dome arches are filled with three rows of windows. To north and south high triple arcades, each supported on two great granite columns, open into side aisles with galleries above, each of three domed bays – but these galleries reach only to the springing of the dome arches. The plan thus gives a sense of an unlimited space filled with light. The *mimber* is a fine work of white marble with a beautiful medallion perforated like an iron grille. The voussoirs of the gallery arches are fretted polychrome of verd antique and Proconessian marble. Altogether Mihrimah Sultan Camii ranks among the very finest mosques in the city, one of Sinan's masterpieces.

## THE SELIMIYE

Sinan continued as chief architect under Süleyman's son and successor, Selim II, who reigned from 1566-74. Thirty of Sinan's extant structures were built during this period, his major project being the Selimiye in Edirne, the imperial mosque complex that he built for the sultan from 1568-75, finished the year after Selim's death. The Selimiye dominates Edirne from an eminence on the east side of town, built on a platform called Kavak Meydaní, the Square of the Poplar. The mosque and its *avlu*, which are identical rectangles in form, 60 metres wide by 44 metres long, are situated toward the northern end of this platform, with the *medrese* of the *külliye* occupying the south-east corner of the precincts and the *dar-ül hadis* the south-west corner. The western side of the precinct is taken up by a commercial building called the Kavaflar Arasta, or Cobblers' Arcade, whose 124 shops were once occupied by the guild of shoemakers, with a *dar-ül kura* projecting from the middle of its outer side. The

Kavaflar Arasta and *dar-ül kura* are believed to be additions founded by Murat III and built for him by Davut Aga, Sinan's successor as chief architect.

The Selimiye is surmounted by its great dome, ringed round with eight turreted weight-towers and framed by its four slender minarets, the tallest in Islam, measuring 70.9 metres from the ground to the tops of their finials. The weight-towers are the projections of the eight octagonal piers that provide the main internal support for the great dome, which is flanked at the corners by semicircular exedrae, with a semicircular apse on the south containing the *mihrab*. The poet Mustafa Sa'i, in his inscription on the graveyard garden of the Süleymaniye, quotes Sinan's boast that his great dome at the Selimiye surpassed that of Haghia Sophia: "Those who consider themselves architects among the Christians say that in the Realm of Islam no dome can equal that of Haghia Sophia; they claim that no Islamic architect would be able to build such a large dome. In this mosque, with the help of Allah and the support of Sultan Selim Khan, I erected a dome six cubits wider and four cubits higher than the dome of Haghia Sophia." (A cubit equals 0.5 metres.)

But Sinan's claim is not quite valid, for the slightly elliptical dome of Haghia Sophia has an average diameter of 31.35 metres, whereas that of the Selimyiye is 31.28 metres. Also, the dome of the Selimiye measures 43.5 metres from the floor to the crown, whereas that of Haghia Sophia is 55.6 metres. But the important thing is not whether Sinan could build a dome higher and wider than that erected by Justinian's architects. It is that in developing classical Ottoman architecture to its logical conclusion he could design and build an edifice that compared in its grandeur with the great Byzantine cathedral. Two of the huge dome piers flank the main entryway from the *avlu* and two others flank the *mihrab*. The *müezzin*'s tribune is in the centre of the prayer room, directly beneath the great dome; this is a marble platform carried on rectangular columns and surmounting a marble patio with a pretty fountain at its centre, an arrangement unique in Ottoman architecture. The *mihrab* is also of marble, as is the *mimber*, perhaps the finest in all of Turkey, with its sides carved in a striking openwork design. The lower walls of the *mihrab* apse are revetted in fine Iznik tiles, above which there is a calligraphic inscription with flowing white letters on a blue ground. In the south-west corner the imperial loge is carried out from the east gallery on a portico with four arches. This is one of the most gorgeous chambers in all of Turkey, for its tile

Behind his mosque, Süleyman had two mausoleums built, for himself and his wife, Roxelana. The sultan's tomb is constructed according to an octagonal plan and capped by two domes, one above the other. One dome is carried in the interior by eight porphyry columns, and the other rests on the outside wall. Two other rulers were subsequently buried in the same *türbe*.

SINAN MADE TWO CONTRIBUTIONS
TO THE TOPKAPÍ SARAYÍ (THE IMPERIAL
RESIDENCE OF THE OTTOMAN SULTANS,
TODAY A MUSEUM). HE WAS RESPONSIBLE
FOR THE MONUMENTAL KITCHENS,
AND HE LATER DESIGNED THIS CEREMONIAL
HALL, CALLED THE CHAMBER OF
MURAT III (1574-95), ENTIRELY BLANKETED
IN CERAMIC TILES, ONE WALL OF THE
CHAMBER IS ALSO DECORATED
BY A FOUNTAIN.

decoration is absolutely unsurpassed in any other mosque in the country, or even in Topkapí Sarayí (the imperial residence of the Ottoman sultans). The *mihrab* in the imperial loge is extraordinary, too, for at its centre two superb wooden shutters open to reveal a window looking out over Edirne and its surrounding countryside.

## THE LAST MOSQUES

During the 1570s, when he spent most of his time working on the Selimiye, Sinan also built four mosques for Sokollu Mehmet Pasha, who in the years 1564-79 served as grand vezir under Süleyman, Selim II and Murat III. The first mosque that Sinan built for Sokollu Mehmet was at Lüleburgaz (1569-70) in Thrace, the second was at Kadirga Liman in Istanbul (1571-72), the third at Payas (1574-75) on the eastern Mediterranean coast of Anatolia, and the fourth at Azap Kapí in Galata (1577-78). The most renowned of these is the one at Kadirga Liman, on the Marmara slope of the First Hill. This mosque was founded by Sokollu Mehmet Pasha in honour of his wife, Esmahan Sultan, daughter of Selim II. The entrance to the mosque courtyard is unique, the outer gateway being beneath the large domed chamber that served as the *dershane* of the *medrese*. A flight of steps ascends from there to the *avlu*, which is centred on a domed *sadírvan* with widely overhanging eaves. The domed cells of the *medrese*, sixteen in all, are arrayed around three sides of the courtyard, the portico being completed on the fourth side by the seven-bayed porch of the mosque, whose entryway faces the *dershane* and its underlying staircase. In the lunettes of the mosque windows under the porch there are some striking and elegant inscriptions in blue and white faience. The internal plan of the mosque is a hexagon inscribed in an almost square rectangle, with the central area covered by a dome, counter-balanced at the corners by four small semidomes. There are no side aisles, but around three sides there is a low gallery supported on slender marble columns with typical Ottoman lozenge capitals. The polychrome of the arches, whose voussoirs are of alternate red and green marble, is characteristic of the period. The tile decoration of the mosque has been done with singularly charming effect. Only selected areas of the walls have been sheathed in tiles: the pendentives below the dome, a frieze of floral design, and the exquisite central section of the east wall. The central panel frames the *mihrab* with tiles decorated in vine and floral motifs in turquoise on a background of pale green, interspersed with panels of fine calligraphy with white letters on a deep-blue field. The finely carved marble *mimber* is surmounted by a tall conical cap, sheathed in the same turquoise tiles that frame the *mihrab*. Above the *mihrab* the framed arch in the east wall is pierced by elegant stained-glass windows, whose spectrum of bright colours complements the cool tones of the faience flowers below. Above the entrance portal one can see a small specimen of the wonderful painted decoration of the classical period, of which only a very few examples remain in Istanbul. It consists of very elaborate arabesque designs in rich and varied colours.

Other extant structures by Sinan from the reign of Selim II are Sokollu Mehmet Pasha's *türbe* and *medrese* at Eyüp on the Golden Horn (1568-69); Semiz Ali Pasha Camii in Babaeski (1569); Piyale Pasha Camii at Kasím Pasha near Galata (1573-74); and Mimar Sinan Mescidi, his own foundation at Karagümrük in Istanbul (1573-74). During that period Sinan made extensive repairs on Haghia Sophia, erecting two minarets (1573), and he also restored Topkapí Sarayí, adding the huge kitchens (1573-74) that are now the *saray*'s principal landmark as seen from the Marmara shore. Sinan continued to serve as chief architect under Murat III, Selim II's son, who became sultan after his father's death in 1574. Sinan's output continued to be prodigious in the fourteen years that were left to him before his death in 1588, and 44 extant structures are listed for him in this period. These include Sokollu Kasim Pasha Camii at Havsa (1576-77); the *türbe* of Selim II at Haghia Sophia (1576-77); the Salon of Murat III in Topkapí Sarayí (1578-79); Atik Valide Camii in Üsküdar (1579-83); Zal Mahmut Pasha Camii in Eyüp (circa 1580); Kílíç Ali Pasha Camii on the Bosphorus at Tophane (1580-81); Semsi Pasha Camii on the Bosphorus at Üsküdar (1580-81); Mesih Pasha Camii on the Fourth Hill in Istanbul (1585-86), and Ramazan Efendi Camii on the Seventh Hill (1585-86). Nisancí Mehmet Pasha Camii on the Fourth Hill in Istanbul (1588) is also attributed to Sinan, in which case it would have been his last mosque, completed when he was at least 93.

Atik Valide Camii was founded by the Valide Sultan (Queen Mother) Nur Banu, wife of Selim II and mother of Murat III; her mosque stands at the summit of a hill high on the Asian shore of the Bosphorus near the end of the strait, dominating the skyline of Üsküdar. This is the most splendid and extensive of all Sinan's constructions in Istanbul, with the sole exception of the Süleymaniye. In addition to the mosque itself, the *külliye* consists of a *medrese*, a hospital, an *imaret*, a *dar-ül kura*, a caravanserai, and a *hamam*; all these buildings are still in existence and most are in good condition. Atik

Valide Camii is preceded by one of the most beautiful of all the mosque courtyards, a grandly proportioned cloister with domed porticoes supported on marble columns. In the centre are the *sardírvan* and many ancient plane trees and cypresses. The mosque is entered through an elaborate double porch, the outer one with a penthouse roof, the inner domed and with handsome tiled inscriptions over the windows. Inside, one finds a wide rectangular room with a central dome supported by a hexagonal arrangement of pillars and columns. There are galleries around three sides of the room, and the wooden ceilings under some of them preserve that rich painting typical of the period: floral and arabesque designs in black, red and gold. The *mihrab* is in a square projecting apse revetted in magnificent tiles of the best Iznik period; the window-frames are of deep-red conglomerate marble with shutters richly inlaid with mother-of-pearl. The *mihrab* and *mimber* are fine works in carved marble.

The Salon of Murat III, which Sinan completed just before he began work on Atik Valide Camii, is the grandest of all the rooms in Topkapí Sarayí, particularly since it retains the whole of its original decoration by Sinan. The walls are sheathed in Iznik tiles of their greatest period; the panel of plum blossoms surrounding the elegant bronze chimney-piece is especially noteworthy, as is the calligraphic frieze that runs around the room. Opposite the fireplace is an elaborate three-tiered fountain of carved polychrome marble set in a marble embrasure. But it is the perfect and harmonious proportions of the room, as much as its superb decoration, that lend it distinction and charm, another of Sinan's masterpieces.

Another of Sinan's late works is the little complex that he built for himself opposite the north-west corner of the Süleymaniye precinct wall, a triangular site with a marble sebil at its apex and the three walls enclosing a graveyard. Just within the angle of the apex is Sinan's own *türbe*. The *türbe* stands in what was once the garden of Sinan's house, which he built when he began working on the Süleymaniye in 1550 and lived in for the rest of his life when he was not engaged in projects outside Istanbul. Sinan's *türbe* is an open structure: an arcade with six ogive arches supports a marble roof with a tiny dome over his marble sarcophagus, surmounted by a stone tombstone in the form of the great turban that he wore as Chief of the Imperial Architects. On the south wall of the graveyard there is a long inscription by Sinan's friend, the poet Mustafa Sa'i, written in praise of the great architect's accomplishments. It is indeed fitting that Sinan should

CERAMIC PANELS QUOTING EXTRACTS FROM THE KORAN (OPPOSITE) ARE SET AT INTERVALS ALONG THE PASSAGES THAT LEAD TO ROOMS DEVOTED TO MEDITATION AND PRAYER, IN THE SIDE AISLES OFF THE MOSQUE'S CENTRAL PRAYER ROOM.

be buried here, within close view of the Süleymaniye, the majestic monument with which he crowned the golden age of Süleyman the Magnificent.

## THE OTTOMAN RENAISSANCE

Classical Ottoman architecture had already begun its evolution before Sinan appeared upon the scene, though he was the overwhelming influence in developing it to its logical conclusion. The first Osmanlí mosques of the thirteenth century were in the form of domed cubes, where the concept of centrality and verticality was already clearly evident, as opposed to the horizontality of Selçuk and Arab mosques with their great flat-roofed prayer rooms and their forests of pillars. As the Osmanlí state expanded from a tiny *beylik* (principality) into a world empire, the domed cube grew apace, the imperial architects striving to produce monumental mosques of appropriate size and grandeur. This development was heightened by the Turkish conquest of Constantinople in 1453, when Fatih found himself heir to the eastern dominions of the Roman Empire, with the conquest of southern Europe already underway. The very day that he entered Constantinople, Fatih ordered Haghia Sophia converted into a mosque, and the first Muslim service was held there the following Friday. The ancient cathedral of Constantinople became the first imperial mosque in Istanbul, and thus all subsequent foundations by Fatih and his successors would be profoundly influenced by Haghia Sophia, particularly by the hovering presence of its great dome. When the Conqueror built his own imperial mosque on the Fourth Hill, the original Fatih Camii, he had his architect create for him an edifice that strongly resembled Haghia Sophia, according to the testimony of both Turkish and Western observers. His son and successor, Beyazit II, also used Haghia Sophia as an archetype in building his imperial mosque complex, the Beyazidiye, as did Süleyman in completing the mosque that he dedicated to his father, Selim I. This was the architectural heritage that Sinan would have become aware of when he first came out of Karamania as a young Janissary cadet, seeing the great domed edifice of Haghia Sophia and the imperial mosques of Fatih, Beyazit II and Selim I, then later the monuments of all the countries through which he travelled during seven campaigns of Süleyman. Although Sinan took part in the expedition to Apulia in 1537, he never travelled in Italy, nor is it likely that he was aware of the architectural concepts that were being developed in the Italian Renaissance, for his very practical education as a Janissary cadet would not have prepared him to read such works as "De re Aedificatori" by Leon Battista Alberti, based on "De Architectura" by Vitruvius. Fatih, who had been tutored in both Greek and Latin, had some idea of what was happening in Italian art, as evidenced by the fact that he invited three Italian painters to decorate Topkapí Sarayí and had his portrait painted by one of them, Gentile Bellini. He also supported the work of both Greek and Turkish scholars in his court and discussed Christianity with Gennadios Scholarios, the first Greek Orthodox Patriarch of Constantinople after the conquest, leading Machiavelli to suggest that the Conqueror was a true Renaissance prince. Beyazit II made unsuccessful overtures to both Leonardo da Vinci and Michelangelo to design a bridge across the Golden Horn, indicating that he was aware of the stature of Italian artists and architects. But although Sinan may not have had a formal knowledge of the theoretical concepts of Western architecture at the time, his own practical experience as an architect of genius in a dynamic new empire expanding into both Asia and Europe made him a true man of the Renaissance, as manifested in his building of the Süleymaniye and the Selimiye. Sinan's knowledge of Ottoman architecture came from two centuries of Turkish building practices and from his observations of Byzantine edifices, above all from the archetype of Haghia Sophia.

Sinan, in his post as Chief of the Imperial Architects, had all of the vast resources of the mighty Ottoman Empire behind him, so that he could complete his most monumental projects in a remarkably short time, the principal reason for his extraordinarily prolific output. As Aptullah Kuran points out: "Considering that the St. Peter's Cathedral in Rome took 160 years from Bramante to Bernini, and that Sir Christopher Wren worked for 40 years on St. Paul's in London, the completion of the Istanbul Süleymaniye in seven and the Edirne Selimiye in six years shows the wealth of the Empire and the speed and efficiency with which the Corps of Court Architects performed their duty." ("Sinan, the Grand Old Master of Ottoman Architecture", Washington, D.C., and Istanbul, 1987.) Sinan's career coincided with the apogee of Ottoman power, which waned in the century after Süleyman's death. The creative force of Turkish architects declined along with the fortunes of the empire, and after Sinan's death Ottoman architecture never again brought forth a masterpiece comparable to those that were created by Sinan. Three centuries after the passing of Sinan, his edifices stand out as the supreme monuments of the Ottoman Empire, immortalising the architect of Süleyman's golden age.

T HE ART OF OTTOMAN CERAMICS

EVOLVED QUICKLY IN THE SIXTEENTH

CENTURY WITH THE DISCOVERY,

IN MID-CENTURY, OF A VIVID TOMATO-RED

COLOUR IN THE IZNIK WORKSHOPS.

FOR A BRIEF PERIOD – BEFORE THE SECRET

OF ITS PRODUCTION WAS LOST

AT THE END OF THE CENTURY – WALLS

WERE REFACED WITH STUNNINGLY

BEAUTIFUL FLORAL DESIGNS DOMINATED

BY RED AND BLUE.

THE IMPERIAL OTTOMAN TOMBS DISPLAY

THE UTMOST DEGREE OF ARTISTIC

PERFECTION. THE TILES DO NOT BEAR

IDENTICAL PATTERNS, BUT FORM LARGE

COMPOSITIONS SIMILAR TO THOSE

OF PRAYER RUGS, SYMBOLISING PARADISE,

THE ABODE OF DEAD SULTANS' SOULS.

THE PINNACLE OF THIS ART FORM

(OPPOSITE) IS THE *TÜRBE* OF SELIM II

(1566-74), ERECTED IN THE PRECINCT OF

HAGHIA SOPHIA (AND FINISHED IN 1577).

P

RAISE BE TO ALLAH,
THE INCOMPARABLE
CREATOR ... WHO CREATED
THE TERRESTRIAL GLOBE
WITH NEITHER ARCHITECT
NOR MASON, NEITHER
PILLAR NOR SUPPORT.

*SINAN*

A STAIRWAY OPENING ONTO THE *AVLU*
(FORECOURT) OF THE SOKOLLU MEHMET
PASHA CAMII (PAGE 50). THE MONUMENTAL
*AVLU* SURROUNDED BY PORTICOES IS A
FEATURE EXCLUSIVE TO IMPERIAL
MOSQUES. ABOVE: THE *AVLU* OF THE
SEHZADE MEHMET CAMII, BUILT BY SINAN
IN 1548 FOR SÜLEYMAN, TO HONOUR HIS
SON'S MEMORY. OPPOSITE, THE ABLUTIONS
FOUNTAIN AND *AVLU* OF THE SÜLEYMANIYE
*KÜLLIYE*. THE MOSQUE WAS COMPLETED IN
1557, THE OTHER BUILDINGS LATER.

O TTOMAN ARCHITECTURE IS EPITOMISED

BY THE DIVERSE MEANS IT DEVISED TO

COVER SIMILARLY PROPORTIONED,

BUT VARIOUSLY SIZED, SPACES WITH

SYSTEMS OF DOMES. PRECEDING PAGES:

THE *AVLU* FAÇADE OF THE SÜLEYMANIYE.

ABOVE: A DETAIL OF THE AZAP KAPÍ CAMII,

BUILT IN 1577-78 FOR SOKOLLU MEHMET

PASHA IN THE AZAP KAPÍ QUARTER OF

ISTANBUL. OPPOSITE: THE *AVLU* FAÇADE OF

THE SEHZADE MEHMET CAMII.

**D**ETAIL OF A FOUNTAIN WITH
POLYCHROME, OR MANY-COLOURED,
RELIEFS IN THE OUTER PRECINCT OF THE
ŞEHZADE MEHMET CAMII, WHICH WAS
BUILT IN MEMORY OF SÜLEYMAN'S ELDEST
SON. BEHIND THE FOUNTAIN IS AN
ENTRANCE TO THE *AVLU.*

ONE CAN TELL THAT THIS ROOF COVERS
AN *AVLU* BY ITS DOUBLE SERIES OF DOMES.
FURTHERMORE, ONE CAN DETERMINE THAT
IT IS AN *AVLU* OF A *MEDRESE* (THEOLOGICAL
SCHOOL) BY THE CHIMNEYS, WHICH
CORRESPOND TO THE FIREPLACES
IN THE STUDENTS' ROOMS.

THE *AVLU* (FORECOURT) OF AN IMPERIAL

MOSQUE WAS PROBABLY THE SCENE OF

A RITUAL, WHOSE NATURE IS UNKNOWN TO

US TODAY. IN THE SÜLEYMANIYE, THE

PRESENCE OF THE ABLUTIONS FOUNTAIN

HAS WHAT APPEAR TO BE SYMBOLIC

ORIGINS. THE FAITHFUL PERFORMED THEIR

ABLUTIONS AT TAPS SET INTO THE

MOSQUE'S LATERAL FAÇADE.

ISLAM STRICTLY PRESCRIBES RITUAL
ABLUTIONS BEFORE THE FIVE DAILY
PRAYERS; THUS THE *SADIRVAN*,
OR ABLUTIONS FOUNTAIN, OCCUPIES
A PROMINENT PLACE IN THE *AVLU*.
ABOVE: THE FOUNTAIN OF THE KİLİÇ ALİ
PASHA CAMII, ERECTED AROUND 1580.
OPPOSITE: THE FOUNTAIN AT THE MOSQUE
OF SOKOLLU MEHMET PASHA, BUILT
IN THE LITTLE TOWN OF LÜLEBURGAZ,
BETWEEN EDIRNE AND ISTANBUL.

A MONG THE DECORATIVE ELEMENTS
OF A MOSQUE'S FAÇADES, THE
ORNAMENTAL STRINGCOURSES THAT RUN
ALONG THE WALLS AND LINK THE VARIOUS
COMPONENTS OF THE BUILDING PLAY
A MAJOR ROLE. FOLLOWING PAGES: A
DETAIL OF THE *TÜRBE* OF PRINCE
MEHMET AT THE SEHZADE.

NTRICATE STALACTITES ARE ANOTHER
ESSENTIAL DECORATIVE ELEMENT
OF THE OTTOMAN MOSQUE. USED BOTH
INSIDE AND OUT, THESE RICHLY CARVED
CORBELS ARE BUILT WITHIN INTERIOR
ANGLES – HENCE THEIR FREQUENT USE
IN PORTALS, WHERE THEY SOMETIMES SEEM
TO ASSUME THE SHAPE OF STRANGE
MYTHICAL BEINGS.

PILASTERS ROUND OFF THE CORNERS
OF VERTICAL RIBS. SOME (ABOVE) ARE
ACTUALLY SMALL COLUMNS FASHIONED
IN PRECIOUS MARBLE; OTHERS (OPPOSITE)
ARE SCULPTED DECORATIONS. PAGE 70:
DOORS, ORNAMENTED WITH SUCH RICH
MATERIALS AS MOTHER-OF-PEARL,
TORTOISE SHELL, IVORY AND EBONY,
DISPLAY BRILLIANTLY CONCEIVED
GEOMETRIC DESIGNS.

What is required
is a silent place with a face
turned toward Mecca.
The space must be vast
so that the heart may feel
at ease; and high,
so that prayers
have air to breathe.
*Le Corbusier*
*Le Voyage d'Orient, 1911*

THE SÜLEYMANIYE. THE PRINCIPAL
BEAUTY OF A MOSQUE'S INTERIOR LIES
IN ITS SPATIAL UNITY, WHICH REFLECTS
THE ONENESS OF GOD AND, FOR THE
OTTOMANS, THE ONENESS OF THE EMPIRE
AND ITS SOVEREIGN. AS OTTOMAN
RELIGIOUS ARCHITECTURE EVOLVED, THE
PIERS AND PILLARS THAT CHARACTERISED
THE ARAB HYPOSTYLE MOSQUE WERE
ELIMINATED IN FAVOUR OF A SINGLE
DOME, WHICH CONSIDERABLY ENLARGED
THE CENTRAL SPACE.

IN THE SÜLEYMANIYE, THE GENERAL
PLAN AND THE WAY THE WEIGHT OF THE
DOME IS DISTRIBUTED ARE DELIBERATELY
PATTERNED AFTER HAGHIA SOPHIA.
THE THRUST OF THE GREAT DOME, WHICH
RESTS UPON FOUR PIERS, IS ABSORBED
BY TWO SEMIDOMES SITUATED IN THE AXIS
OF THE PRAYER HALL, AN ARRANGEMENT
WHICH ALLOWED SPACE ON THE SIDES FOR
NON-LOAD-BEARING WALLS WITH A
MULTITUDE OF WINDOWS.

THE LATERAL THRUST OF THE GREAT
SÜLEYMANIYE DOME IS NOT ABSORBED
BY BUTTRESSES BUT RATHER, AS IN A
CHRISTIAN BASILICA, BY SIDE AISLES
TO THE LEFT AND RIGHT OF THE CENTRAL
SPACE. THIS INFRINGEMENT OF THE RULE
OF A SINGLE LARGE PRAYER ROOM
ALLOWED SINAN TO CREATE QUIET SPACES
FOR MEDITATION AND FOR THE READING
AND TEACHING OF THE KORAN.

Ottoman stained-glass windows differ from Western ones in two ways: the skeleton is plaster, and representation of the human form is prohibited. Yet the aim is the same: to filter light entering the sanctuary, and to allow larger openings than could be filled with single spans of glass. OPPOSITE: THE RIGHT WING OF THE SÜLEYMANIYE, VISIBLE BEHIND A SUPERB SCREEN OF OPENWORK, WAS USED AS A LIBRARY.

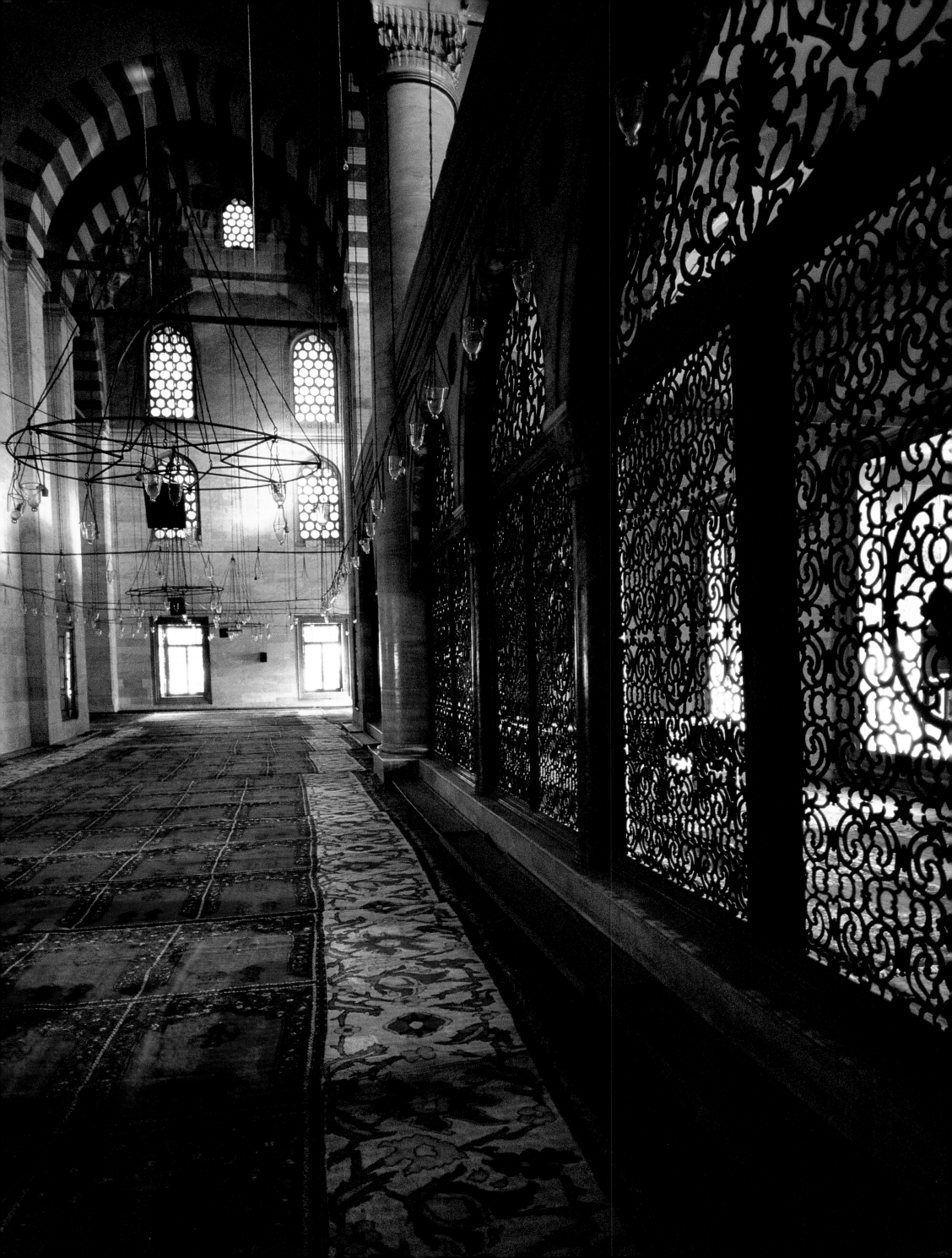

Among the achievements of Sinan's masterpiece, the Selimiye in Edirne (above, opposite and on the preceding pages), are its absolute spatial unity, its 31.28-metre dome, and its rare luminosity, attributable to the virtual absence of supporting walls. The dome rests – with neither semidomes nor pendentives, but only a few stalactites – upon an octagon supported by eight piers.

Your servant was challenged by the claim that it was a difficult task to create such a dome. In this mosque, with the help of Almighty Allah and the support of Sultan Selim Khan, I proved my ability and erected a dome six cubits wider and four cubits higher than that of Haghia Sophia. (From 'Tezkiret ül-Bünyan', a biography of Sinan written circa 1586 by the poet Mustafa Sa'i.)

THE SELIMIYE'S NEED FOR HUGE
BUTTRESSES, AND THE ARCHITECT'S DESIRE
TO CONCEAL THEIR PRESENCE ON THE
FAÇADE, RESULTED IN RESIDUAL SPACE
THAT WAS TRANSFORMED INTO GALLERIES
(ABOVE AND ON THE FOLLOWING PAGES).
THESE HIDDEN AREAS, REACHED BY
FLIGHTS OF STEPS CARVED INTO THE WALLS
AND CONNECTED BY PASSAGES IN THE
BUTTRESSES, EMPHASISE THE VASTNESS
OF THE CENTRAL SPACE.

WHEN THE EYE GROWS ACCUSTOMED
TO THE IMMENSITY OF THE SELIMIYE
MOSQUE'S INTERIOR, IT CAN LINGER OVER
THE WEALTH OF FASCINATING DETAILS.
THE SPRINGING OF AN ARCH TO A PILLAR
VIA AN INTRICATE STALACTITE, THE
EMBRASURES OF THE FLOOR-LENGTH
WINDOWS, THE HARMONY OF A FOUNTAIN,
A BALUSTRADE DIVIDING TWO
LEVELS – ALL OF THESE CONTRIBUTE
TO ITS DIGNIFIED BEAUTY.

CUT-OFF CORNERS, MOULDINGS, NICHES,
BALUSTRADES AND DECORATIVE FRAMES
OVER ARCHWAYS, ALL CROWNED BY
VERSES FROM THE KORAN, IN THE
SELIMIYE'S LONG SERIES OF GALLERIES.
OPPOSITE: THE SELIMIYE POSSESSES
A FEATURE UNIQUE IN OTTOMAN
ARCHITECTURE – A FOUNTAIN SITUATED
IN THE CENTRE OF THE MOSQUE, UNDER
THE *MÜEZZIN MAHFILI* (TRIBUNE
FOR THE *MÜEZZIN*).

IN THE MOSQUE OF SÜLEYMAN'S
DAUGHTER, PRINCESS MIHRIMAH,
(FOLLOWING PAGES), SINAN ELIMINATED
CORNER PIERS, RELEGATING THEM TO
THE OUTSIDE OF THE MOSQUE. THE DOME
RESTS ON FOUR ELEGANT PENDENTIVES,
WHICH SEEM TO MELT AWAY IN THE LIGHT
FLOODING FROM WALLS THAT NO LONGER
SUPPORT ANY WEIGHT. THE DOME
APPEARS SUSPENDED, LIKE THE CANOPY
OF HEAVEN. PAGES 96-97: THE *MIMBER*
(PULPIT) OF THE MIHRIMAH SULTAN CAMII.

Sinan constantly sought new approaches to architectural problems posed by the mosques he built for the Empire's high dignitaries. Opposite: the Azap Kapí Camii resembles the Selimiye, writ small. Above: a mosque in Havsa (also created for Sokollu Mehmet Pasha), has a square plan. Following pages: the mosque of the high admiral Piyale Pasha follows the archaic style, with six domes on two piers.

For the mosque of high admiral Kílíç Ali Pasha (pages 102-103), erected in 1580 in the Tophane district of Istanbul, Sinan copied exactly the model of Haghia Sophia. Opposite: perhaps to enlarge the prayer room even more, he added galleries modelled on the gynaeceum of the Christian basilica. Above: this mosque is also famed for its lovely stained-glass windows.

THE MESIH PASHA CAMII (PAGES 106-107
AND 108-109) WAS BUILT IN 1585. THOUGH
OVER NINETY YEARS OLD AT THE TIME,
SINAN WAS SURROUNDED BY A TEAM OF
ARCHITECTS WHO IMPLEMENTED HIS
DESIGNS – IN THIS CASE, THE OCTAGONAL
MODEL OF THE SELIMIYE. ABOVE:
THE FINEST STRUCTURE IN THE SEHZADE
*KÜLLIYE* (THE MOSQUE COMPLEX), THE
*TÜRBE* OF THE DEAD PRINCE.

IN 1560 RÜSTEM PASHA, GRAND VEZIR
AND HUSBAND OF SÜLEYMAN'S DAUGHTER
MIHRIMAH, HAD A MOSQUE BUILT IN
ISTANBUL'S LIVELIEST DISTRICT, ON THE
BANKS OF THE GOLDEN HORN (ABOVE AND
ON THE PRECEDING PAGE). THE INTERIOR
IS BLANKETED IN CERAMIC TILES. INDEED,
THE BEAUTIFULLY CONSERVED MOSQUE IS
A VERITABLE MUSEUM OF SIXTEENTH-
CENTURY OTTOMAN CERAMICS.

THOUGH IT IS NOT LARGE, THE RÜSTEM

PASHA CAMII (ABOVE AND ON THE

FOLLOWING PAGES) CONVEYS AN

IMPRESSION OF GRANDEUR OWING TO

SINAN'S ORIGINAL USE OF A DOME RESTING

ON AN OCTAGON. CERAMIC TILES COVER

THE WALLS UP TO THE BASE OF THE DOME.

TILES OF VARYING SHAPES WERE USED

ON LARGE AREAS, ON DOOR AND WINDOW

FRAMES, AND ON THE TRIANGLES

BETWEEN THE ARCHES.

IN THE SEHZADE MEHMET CAMII,
SINAN TOOK THE PLAN OF HAGHIA SOPHIA
TO ITS LOGICAL CONCLUSION (OPPOSITE,
ABOVE AND ON THE FOLLOWING PAGES).
INSTEAD OF BUILDING TWO SEMIDOMES
TO SUPPORT THE CENTRAL DOME,
HE ERECTED FOUR, CREATING A PERFECT
SYMMETRY. HOWEVER, THIS DEVICE
ENTAILED THE USE OF FOUR PIERS;
FINDING A WAY TO ELIMINATE THEM LED
SINAN TO EXPLORE NEW APPROACHES
IN HIS LATER WORKS.

An ELEMENTARY GEOMETRY
DISCIPLINES THE MASSES:
SQUARE, CUBE, SPHERE.
THE PLAN IS THAT OF
A RECTANGULAR COMPLEX
WITH A SINGLE AXIS.
*LE CORBUSIER*
*LE VOYAGE D'ORIENT, 1911*

STATICS AND STYLE BY AUGUSTO ROMANO BURELLI

During the life of some architects, there is only enough time for the conception and full flowering of a single idea. This idea necessarily becomes a figurative fixation, consuming all the architect's time and intellectual energy as he strives to exemplify it in his work. The mosques of Sinan reveal such a single-mindedness. For all his long life Sinan was increasingly obsessed by one architectural type: a centralised plan completely covered by a dome, and the vast, unified space it can create. His hundred mosques bear eloquent witness to the infinite variations that can be made on a single, central architectural type.

The greatness of Sinan is fully demonstrated in the constructive and stylistic mastery with which he joined the dome to the rest of the mosque. The dome is not simply supported like one structure atop another, as was the custom during the European Renaissance, but is rather fused into the whole. This fusion is realised in an intermediate region, animated by vaulted arches, pendentives and niches which make the transition from the quiet of the prayer hall to the perfect balance of the dome. In this intermediate region one can see all Sinan's architectural innovations: the delicate fusing of the dome with the prism of the base, the lightening of the pendentives, his use of arches to distribute weight, the hiding of the structural ribs. All these artifices combine to give a sense of space soaring from the floor of the prayer hall to the blind zenith of the dome. The devices used to lighten the gravity of the elevated masses are derived from the traditional architecture of the Ottoman Empire, but the stalactites are used sparingly and other decoration is reduced to a minimum. The statics of the floor plan, the dynamics of the vaulted elements and the "freezing" of the dome are the salient concepts of the architectural mosque-type.

The need for precision and structural clarity drove Sinan, an engineer and architect, to put outside the mosque the supports and buttresses that hold up the great shell of the dome and those of the semidomes. Sinan strove to incorporate these supports as much as possible into the mosque's exterior walls, to blur the distinction between supporting and supported elements. The mosque's interior displays the same intention: The space must be absolute and uninterrupted, from every point of view. Thus the pilasters and columns of the prayer hall must disappear, or be as unobtrusive as possible. Sinan based his works on elementary geometric units seen in the floor plan. In his mosques, the sphere is joined to the cube using different

A SECTION LOOKING TOWARD THE ENTRANCE FAÇADE AND A PLAN OF THE DOME OF THE MIHRIMAH SULTAN CAMII (PAGE 120). ON EITHER SIDE, ONE CAN SEE THE PILLARS THAT CARRY THE DOME, VISIBLE FROM THE OUTSIDE BUT INTEGRATED INTO THE INNER FAÇADE WALL, WHICH IS 5.62 METRES THICK. OPPOSITE: A STUDY OF THE STRUCTURAL FRAMEWORK OF THE MIHRIMAH SULTAN CAMII (TOP) AND A PLAN, INSCRIBED IN RED, OF THE DOME AND BUTTRESSES.

combinations of these units: the rectangle, square and octagon in the Rüstem Pasha Camii (mosque) in Istanbul and the Selimiye in Edirne; the rectangle and hexagon in the Sokollu Mehmet Pasha Camii in Istanbul's Kadirga Liman quarter; the rectangle and square in the Mihrimah Sultan Camii near Istanbul's Edirne Gate.

It is not possible to fully comprehend the versatility of Sinan without seeing his prolific architectural production in the context of the system he so patiently developed. To supervise construction of the numerous works assigned him, he needed a working method to codify his precepts of composition and construction, something that could guide a project hundreds of kilometres away from his Istanbul headquarters. This method – its guiding and compositional principles, as well as its rules of construction (a technology in which he was expert) – is the basis of Sinan's "school" of architecture. It was a school destined to produce an extraordinary flowering of work even after his death, from the Danube to Algeria to India. Sinan's rational approach to construction, reinforced by compositional principles of great Euclidean rigour, enabled him to be continually innovative in his mosques, mausoleums, caravanserais and bridges. Herein lies the fascination and the ongoing relevance of his teachings.

In Islam, the distance between God and man is unchanging. Nothing intervenes or modifies the separation – not even in architecture, with its emphasis on absolute space. This distance is not unsettling. The mosque, as a place of concentration, tends to ease the separation with its evocation of an almost tangible paradise. Nothing better creates a sensation of quiet and restful contemplation than the space inside a mosque. Even without delving deep into Islamic theology, it is possible to comprehend the nature of space unique to a mosque by looking closely at the symbolic elements each must contain. The mosque always has an axis of longitudinal symmetry that extends from the door that opens onto the *avlu* (forecourt) to the opposite wall, indicating the spiritual orientation of the faithful: the direction to Mecca. This axis is simply a function of the mosque's symmetrical composition: No processions are borne along it, nor does it mark a place of any ritual significance. In a mosque there is no movement. One remains still, kneeling in a given spot, and facing in the same direction as one's fellow worshippers – toward Mecca. All the faithful are equidistant from the ritual itself, because this ritual has no physical focal point within the mosque. The interior is simply a place of assembly and spiritual concentration, and the faithful direct their prayers to a place often far beyond the physical walls of their mosque: Mecca. The convergence of religious expression is purely conceptual, spiritual. The absence of a physical reference point is an essential element of the mosque's design. The space is unencumbered by the altars, baptismal fountains and icons typically found in a Christian church. This absence of centres of attraction ensures a homogeneity of concentration and a unanimity of worship unknown in the Christian world. Both Christianity and Islam attach much importance to the place of the Word, but for Islam, its place is the entire mosque. The Word is the sole ritual medium, and the space that houses the Word must perforce be of the maximum unity, an unarticulated whole, visible from all points. The Word renders not only the rite abstract, but also its spatial projection. The *mimber* in a mosque excercises a ritual function similar to that of the ambo or pulpit in a Christian church: It is where the *imam* stands to give the Friday sermon. But in general, the mosque's ritual is not concentrated in a space overseen by a religious custodian. The prayer leader stands or kneels before the other worshippers simply to guide the direction of the Word, not to embody it.

The wall toward which the worshippers face, the one opposite the *avlu* entrance, is called the *kibla*. Its point of contact with the longitudinal axis is marked by a niche, a kind of blocked-up doorway, called the *mihrab*. The *mihrab* is a blind point upon the *kibla*; functionally it is never dominant. To the right, the triangular *mimber* is a small steep staircase finishing in a canopied pulpit. Its curious form seems to exert pressure upon the wall, indicating the direction toward which the faithful should pray.

Despite the presence of *mihrab* and *mimber*, the *kibla* does not differ much from the mosque's other walls. If these did not bear women's galleries or a royal loge (*hünkar mahfili*), the four walls of a Sinan mosque would be nearly identical. The *kibla* has windows like the other walls, but those around *mihrab* and *mimber* are darkened or obscured to keep these features from being inappropriately highlighted.

Given that the Word is the essence of the Islamic rite, and that the liturgy is not centred on a fixed point, the balance of the prayer hall is related only to the direction of prayer. The unity of faithful requires a floor plan either isotropic or slightly wider along one axis (extending the *kibla* and the wall opposite). There is no hierarchy among the

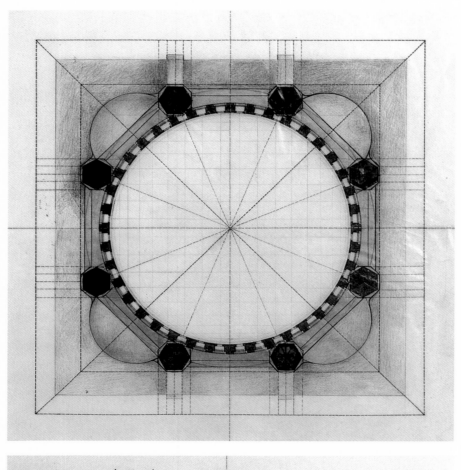

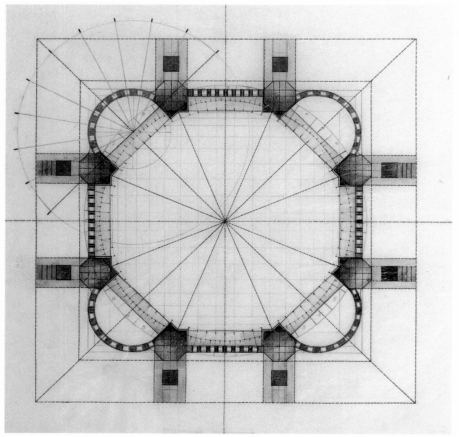

THE SELIMIYE. ABOVE: ARCHITECTURAL
DRAWINGS OF THE OCTAGON (TOP) AND
THE DOME SUPPORTED BY IT. OPPOSITE:
AN OVERVIEW OF THE *KÜLLIYE*. THE
TWO COLLEGES AND THE OUTER PRECINCT
ARE SHADED IN GREEN, THE VERTICAL
SUPPORTS IN VIOLET, THE ARCHES
AND DOMES IN PINK, AND THE DRUM AT
THE BASE OF THE DOME IN RED.

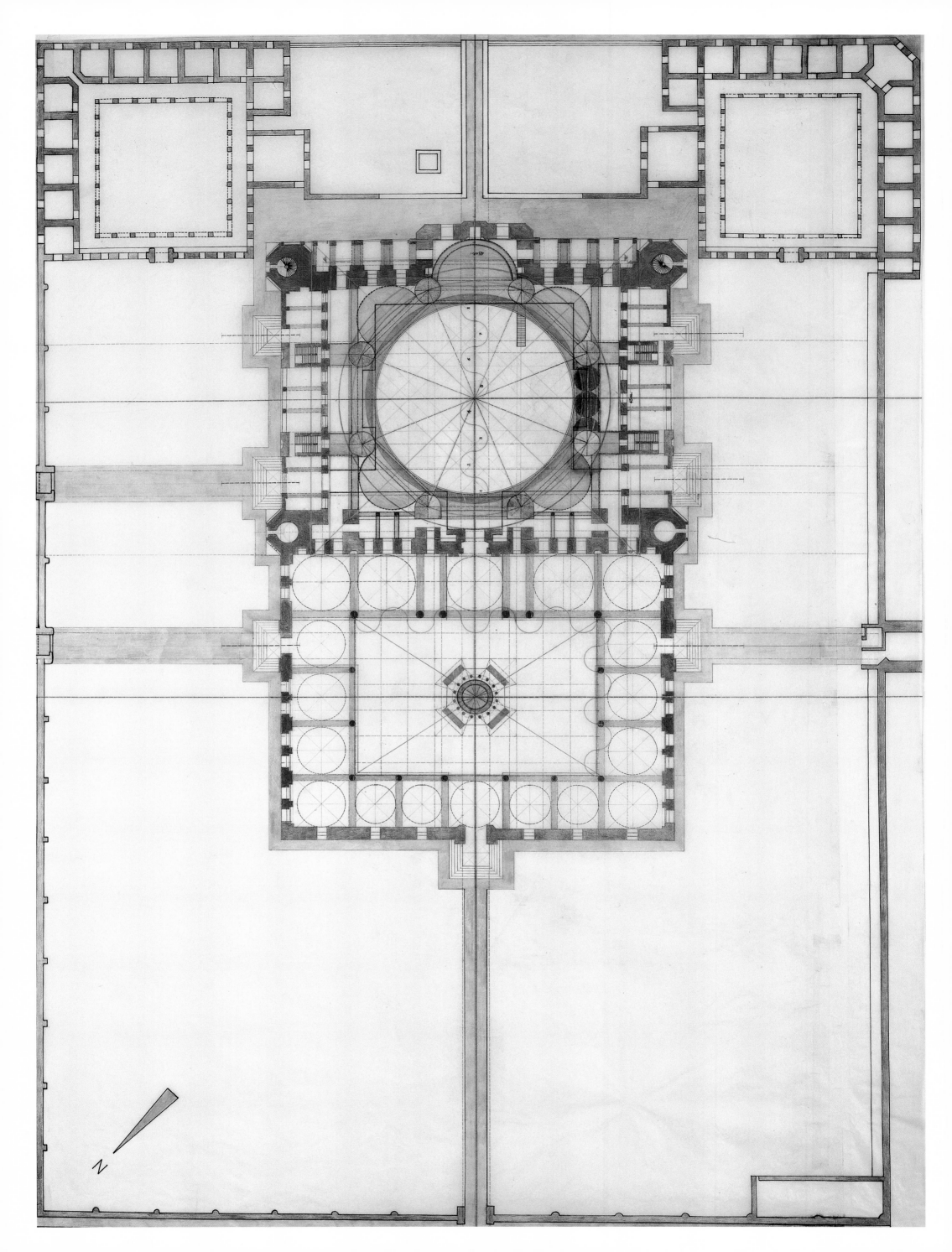

entrances to the hall, although the door that leads to the *avlu* is slightly more decorated than the others, which are located where they will least disturb those at prayer.

The spiritual focus of the rite, a focus whose theological significance goes well beyond the geographic location of Mecca, is represented by an architectural theme that has been present in Islamic tradition from its origins: the dome. As symbol of God's "unity without distinctions", the dome perfectly represents His intangible omnipresence, His formless divinity. The dome unifies a prayer hall whose centre is not physical but cosmic.

The absence of a physical centre, an isotropic prayer space, a direction supplied by the *kibla*, and the dome as cosmic centre – these are the cardinal symbolic elements of the Ottoman mosque. The space of a Sinan mosque is a metaphor for Islamic paradise. Among the ninety-seven Koran verses in which paradise is described, these lines in particular outline the enchantment of the space most strikingly: "As for those who truly fear their Lord, they shall be lodged in towering mansions set about with running streams....those who fear their Lord shall be led in bands to Paradise. When they draw near, its gates will be opened, and its keepers will say to them: 'Peace be to you; you have led good lives. Enter Paradise and dwell in it for ever.' They will say: 'Praise be to God who has made good to us His promise and given us the earth to inherit, that we may dwell in Paradise wherever we please.' Blessed is the reward of the righteous." (The Hordes/Al-Zumar 39:20-73-74. The Koran as translated by N. J. Dawood, Penguin Books, 1990.) This vision of the paradise of life after death – with its abundant water and gates and keepers, where a peaceful, restful truce will reign forever – has ancient origins. In a mosque, the quiet and the free space are contravened only by the direction of prayer. These are the fundamental, unmistakable aspects of the liturgic space. Nothing stands between God and man. Space is suspended in an incomprehensible, unfathomable balance. The prayer hall is free from encumbrances, the supporting structures are invisible, and the dome floating above is worlds away from the static stresses and strains of Western architecture.

The Ottoman dome, as a symbol, is significant – though ambiguous. It is an absolute figure and an emblem of unity. Its zenith is marked by nothing: Projected onto a flat surface, the dome would appear as a circle with no apparent centre. Its points of contact with supporting solids are bathed in light, so that it appears suspended in nothingness, incorporeal. The dome transmits an idea of cosmic order, as immutable as planetary motion. The space it helps define goes far beyond the physical structure of the mosque, which itself is not based on the kind of radial composition that would make the dome its physical centre. The key to the composition of the masses can instead be found among the elementary geometric figures that circle the dome's base, figures which make the transition between the sphere and the prism upon which it sits. The mastery of Sinan lay in his ability to unite the dome with the prism in a way that fuses the two parts into one whole, rather than simply placing one atop the other. The intermediate region in which this fusion takes place forms a kind of "baldachin". It is the centre stage for Sinan's greatest discoveries, all of which contribute to the vision of a unified space rising effortlessly from the floor of the prayer hall to the blind zenith of the dome.

In this intermediate region, Sinan experimented with many structural and stylistic solutions – variations on geometric transitions between the sphere and the cube. As he apparently saw in the Beyazit Camii in Edirne and the Selim I Camii of Istanbul (often mistakenly attributed to Sinan), too abrupt a transition produces the isotropy of the sphere within the cube, the gigantic pendentives reducing the *kibla* to a mere semicircle, thus prescribing the path of prayer. Hence the decision to resolve the conflict between dome and prism above the rectangular room. This passage is gradual, both inside and outside the mosque, and is articulated according to the number of sides on the "baldachin" – for Sinan, four, six or eight. The statics of the prayer hall, the dynamism of the vaulted elements and the "freezing" of the dome – these are the bases for understanding the "suspended space" particular to the mosques created by the master of Istanbul. The space is neither immobile nor inert but is in equilibrium, soaring smoothly past the arches, pendentives and niches toward the halo of windows in the drum at the dome's base.

◆

To understand Sinan's working philosophy, one must put aside the logic of Western composition. In the Renaissance ideal of the relationship between the whole and its parts, the parts obey the *"principium individuationis"*: each clearly states its nature and its role in the whole. The vertical elements (columns, pilasters, pillars) and the horizontal elements (entablatures, fasciae, cornices) work together to explain the

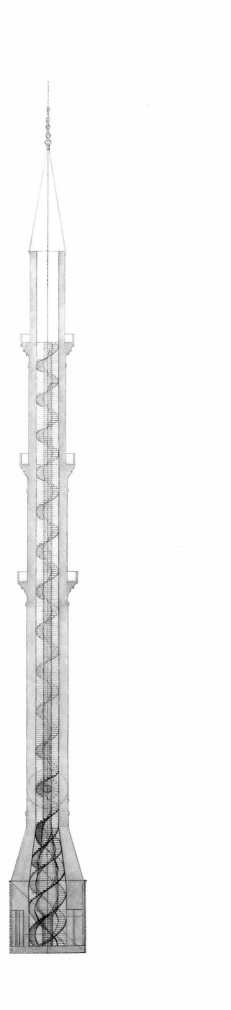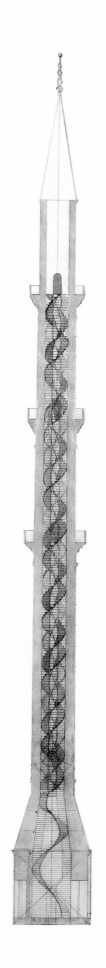

stylistic and static aspects of the structure. The *"principium individuationis"* reinforces the preponderance of the parts over the whole. Suspended loads must therefore show how and by what route they transmit their weight to earth: where and in what way the dome sits upon the baldachin, how the latter's weight is distributed among the arches, where and by what means the transfer occurs between arch and pilaster. Gradation and concatenation are the compositional precepts. But, as Emil Kaufmann says in "Architecture in the Age of Reason, Baroque and Post-Baroque in England, Italy and France" [Cambridge (U.S.A.) 1955], "Gradation is the natural enemy of integration", and gradation usually prevails.

For Sinan, integration generally prevailed over gradation. In his designs, the parts are distinguished by at least a slight autonomy; in some cases they are totally independent and absolutely contrast with the whole, such as in the domed portico at the front of the mosque. Sinan's obsession was the absolute integration of space: Nothing must divide, encumber or fragment it. All must be shown, everything must be perfectly visible from every point of view. In his mosques there are no dark corners or hidden rooms or walkways. To this end, Sinan tended to absorb within the perimeter walls whatever independent elements were imposed by static constraints. This integration hides the forces unleashed in the architectural organism, tending to disperse them rather than concentrate them in pilasters or columns as in Western tradition. But however strong Sinan's aspiration, absolute integration was never fully attainable.

Sinan insisted on a luminous space, an interior filled with an always homogenous light. He knew that buttresses limit the number of potential windows, and that they also cast shadows that cut through the space inside the mosque. For Sinan, the perfect equilibrium of the prayer hall was fully revealed only if light fell uniformly therein. Light fills his mosques, spilling in from all sides and at all levels, from the floor of the faithful to the halo of windows around the tambour at the base of the dome. Of similar shape and size in every wall, the windows are covered by grilles or filled with stained glass, diffusing the incoming light. The space of a Sinan mosque is at the same time metaphysical and profoundly human. Not even its vastness is oppressive. This harmony is made possible by artifice – by decoration, by colouring – but above all, by Sinan's ingenious ways with light. At ground level, the faithful are surrounded by windows that extend up from the floor. The hall is in turn surrounded by a walled garden, enabling

THE FOUR MINARETS OF THE SELIMIYE RISE FROM THE FOUR CORNERS OF THE MOSQUE. OPPOSITE: THE MINARETS THAT FACE THE *AVLU* CONTAIN TRIPLE FLIGHTS OF SPIRAL STEPS, EACH FLIGHT OPENING ONTO A BALCONY.

those at prayer to glance outside at trees, shrubs and flowers. The sense of abstraction is eased, the light and seasonal breezes contribute to an almost domestic impression of peace and tranquillity. The Koranic paradise becomes comprehensible.

Sinan's concept of absolute integration owed much to a tradition that, in his time, was already centuries old. As much as he methodically mapped out how to achieve this integration, the tools he used – the compositional rules, the structural artifices, his chosen materials – all belonged to the stylistic apparatus of Islamic tradition, refined almost to its bare essentials. Professor Dogan Kuban has noted that, whereas nearly all the architects of the Italian Renaissance were grounded in the study of painting, and therefore were less than secure when dealing with structural problems, Sinan's background was in military engineering. He knew how to calibrate the necessary thickness of an arch in accordance with the weight it would have to bear. His calculations were empirical but they were well developed, as is attested to by the delicacy and grace of his structures.

It is certain that Sinan based his calculations on net measures, excluding the walls and their thickness. This was the logical way to proceed, firstly because visible architecture is that of net measures, and secondly because the thickness of walls and arches obeys the static and stylistic rules that can be more freely dealt with during the actual construction than during the planning. By subdividing the basic geometric figures – the circle of the dome, the polygon of the baldachin – and employing net measures, the sustaining walls become neutral bands, sometimes excluded from and sometimes included in the envelope. This is a scholarly game governed by Euclidean geometry, not by the harmonic relations so dear to the Renaissance tradition.

There is always conflict between a rectangular prism and a superimposed dome. To resolve it, one may use any of several architectural artifices, all of which help to mediate between circle and rectangle. The dome, which determines all the statics, needs geometrically established supports and a balanced distribution of its weight among arches, pendentives and pilasters. These are the bases for the geometric configurations of the baldachin. To best resolve the conflict between the dome and the rectangular plan preferred by Islamic liturgy, one must design a transitional area or baldachin that avoids dividing the mosque into thirds. The most obvious choice would be a square baldachin flanked by twin lateral semidomes. But this has the

DIAGRAM (OPPOSITE) INDICATING
THE PLACEMENT OF THE THREE
FLIGHTS OF STAIRS IN THE
CONICAL SPACE AT THE BASE
OF THE MINARET.

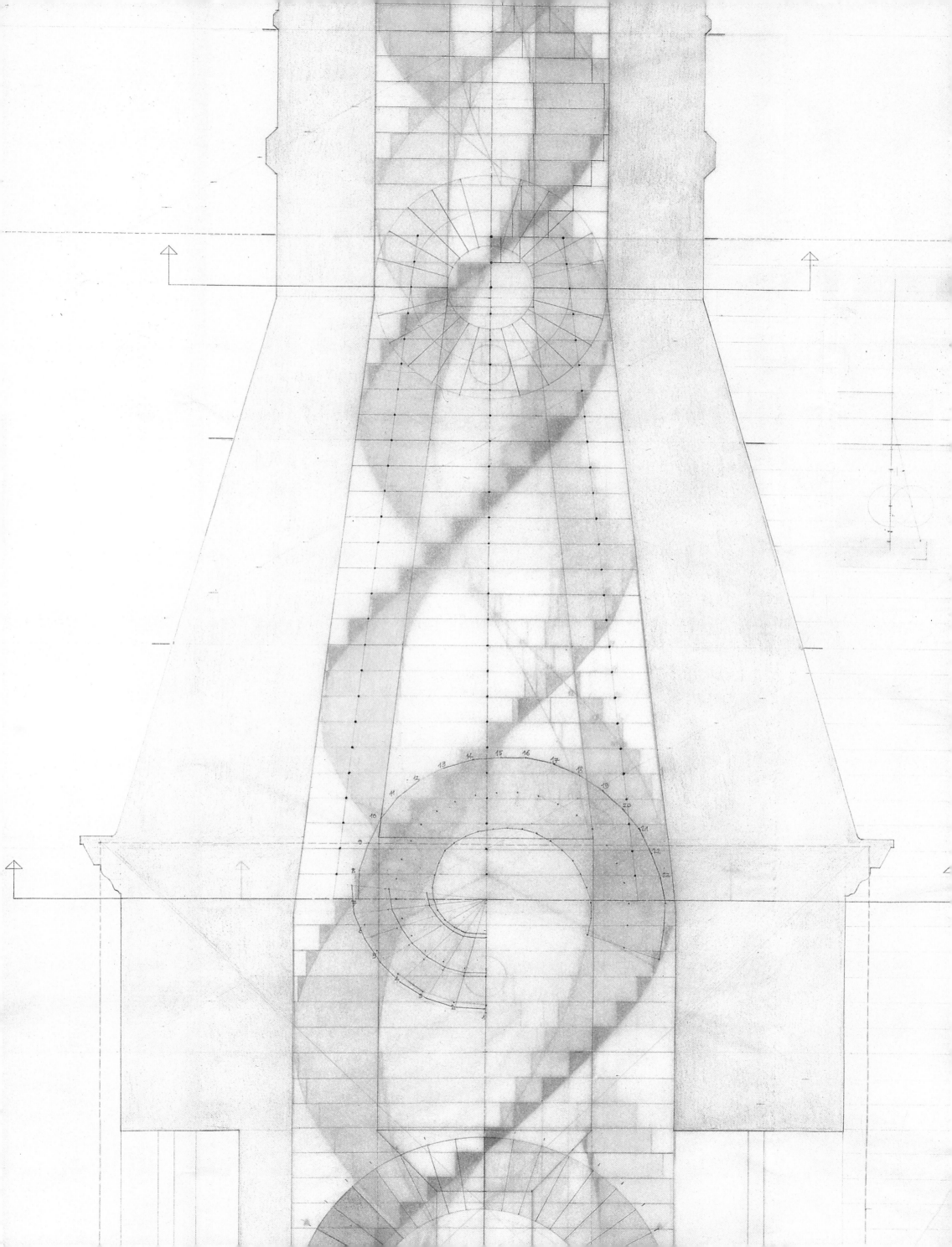

disadvantage of diminishing the relief of the dome, because the twin semidomes have its same diameter. An octagonal baldachin, on the other hand, divides the space into thirds, as illustrated by the Rüstem Pasha Camii. The best solution is a hexagonal baldachin, primarily because a hexagon fits within a rectangle, as it involves a lateral widening. Sinan used the hexagon in such mid-sized mosques as the Sinan Pasha Camii, the Kara Ahmet Pasha Camii, the Semiz Ali Pasha Camii in Babaeski, the Molla Çelebi Camii and the Sokollu Mehmet Pasha Camii. But most of these left unresolved a crucial problem: the relationship between the hall's lateral walls and the baldachin supports. In Sinan's beloved hexagonal baldachin, two of the supporting arches are built within the hall's exterior walls. The other four leave the rectangular plan, joining at two 60° angles that clash with the room's lateral walls. What is missing is a successful collaboration between hall and baldachin supports – a collaboration in the static sense but also, more importantly, in the stylistic.

Only in the Sokollu mosque did Sinan finally achieve an absolute cohesion in the space, which soars unimpeded to the dome. The key to the solution lies in the dynamic articulation of the side walls which contain the central pillars, the tension of the four semidomes, and the two walled arches below them. To obtain the necessary width at the sides, the hexagon is squeezed on the *kibla* side, on which the arches of the baldachin are of slightly different diameter. The room is perfectly open, and the tribunes advance, free and light, concealing the lower part of the pilasters.

In the Mihrimah Sultan Camii at the Edirne Gate, however, Sinan perfected the configuration of a square baldachin by constructing a cubic prism without side semidomes. The four walls, pierced by windows, are actually the filling masonry of the four large arches that distribute the weight of the dome – as well as their own – among four massive supports. The four corner columns are not visible from the interior: the whole baldachin seems to rest on four points, and the pendentives terminate above the coverings of the tribunes. On the exterior, the polygonal pillars become narrower at the very spot where they would be expected to become wider – just below where the arches spring, transforming themselves, with a graceful stalactitic join, into simple pilasters. The raising of a large dome (19.5 metres) above a square baldachin resting on just four supports, despite the fact that it had already been done before Sinan at the Selim I Camii in Istanbul and the Beyazit Camii in Edirne, has never been equalled.

The octagonal baldachin, the most common configuration in Sinan's work, is found in examples ranging from modest structures to the masterpiece of the Selimiye in Edirne. The very nature of this arrangement, which includes at least four supports distinct from the hall's exterior wall, divides the interior into three parts. For the Selimiye, completed in 1575, Sinan erected a dome almost 31.5 metres in diameter, which spans the entire prayer hall, surpassing that of Haghia Sophia (the basilica and masterpiece of Byzantine architecture, completed in 537 in what was then Constantinople) and concluding a challenge begun fifty years earlier. (The Byzantine dome is, in fact, slightly ovoid and thus has both larger and smaller dimensions: It measures 30.9 metres by 31.82 metres.) To erect a dome of such exceptional size, Sinan knew that no matter how thick the perimeter wall, it would not supply the rigidity necessary to neutralise the horizontal thrust. So he built a double diaphragm wall to absorb the deep buttresses. The usage varies on each of the four sides and at different levels: Sometimes the external diaphragm does the work, sometimes the internal. The buttresses are connected to fluted pilasters with a high sculpted arch. The double walls also allowed the stylistic articulation of the mosque's four sides, both inside and out. The pilasters evolve gradually from total autonomy at floor level to total fusion with the baldachin, without extraneous elements such as capitals. The cube of the base intersects the dome at the level of the drum, into which are set forty windows. The sphere of the dome fixes the height of the cornices above the galleries, where the first set of tympanum arches is placed.

◆

Fundamental to understanding Sinan, as well as to clearing up the difference between the stylistic sensibilities of the Islamic world and those of Europe, is the question of "decoration". From the first, "decoration" has meant "to adorn" or "to clothe". In a metaphorical sense, "decoration" refers to ornamentation, especially in rhetoric. But from its origins, the word has carried a semantic ambivalence between the meanings "to clothe by covering" and "to render clear". In the Islamic tradition, the first sense unquestionably prevails over the second. The use of ceramic tiles, sculpted stalactites and painting obviously serves to reclothe an edifice, indeed to transfigure it. August Choisy, a staunch positivist, attempted to explain the stylistic

details of Islamic architecture in terms of practical reasons and customs of construction ("Histoire de l'Architecture", Paris, 1905). But Choisy overlooked the fact that the purpose of decoration is not to elucidate chosen structural details, but rather to mask or blur the construction procedure used. The Ottoman meaning of "decoration" was "transfiguration", not "clarification".

For Sinan, decoration tended to reconcile opposites. He seemed to say: "I will build a perfect machine animated by great constructive energy. But all traces of this energy must disappear: The dome must seem as if suspended, the materials must be hidden by precious coverings." The *muqarnas* (traditional Islamic decorative stalactites), for example, cover the points of the greatest concentration of lines of force (when these are in play outside the vertical plane, as with capitals or pendentives). Sinan sought to camouflage these lines of force, and he did so by employing *muqarnas*. Sculpted in honeycombed shapes, almost dripping from the vertical plane, they give the impression of being suspended. Meanwhile, Sinan used painting and ceramic tiles to form a covering composed of small, brightly coloured motifs repeated on a light background. By thus luminously adorning the walls, he removed any sense of crushing weight. In Sinan's mosques, surfaces of all dimensions are carpeted by painted patterns, by floral or geometric motifs.

◆

The perspective view of space was foreign to Islamic, and in particular to Ottoman, sensibilities. Perspective, with its orchestrated sequences, imposes a predetermined position on the spectator, in effect saying to him: "You must see the object *like this* and in no other way." This emphasises the monumental and ceremonial aspects of an edifice, stressing a theatrical effect. Axes of symmetry are usually those of the visual cone. Moving along such an axis, one is prepared for – indeed expects – a succession of discoveries. The observer, inasmuch as he is guided by the architect's will, is an actor on a stage: he becomes the centre of the architecture, which seems to obey him. None of this happens in an Ottoman mosque. The plan of the *külliye* (the whole mosque complex) shows that the buildings housing the religious institutions that surround the enclosure are arrayed along Cartesian axes – which are the axes of the mosque itself. Nothing is arranged according to rules of perspective. If one looks at the

AXONOMETRIC PROJECTION (OPPOSITE) OF THE MIHRIMAH SULTAN CAMII. THE DOME MEASURES 20 METRES IN DIAMETER, AND ITS HEIGHT FROM THE FLOOR IS 37 METRES. THE THICKNESS OF THE ARCHES, WHEN COMPARED TO THAT OF THE THIN WALL CONTAINING THE WINDOWS, SHOWS THE STATICS SCHEME – HOW THE OPPOSING FORCES ARE IN EQUILIBRIUM.

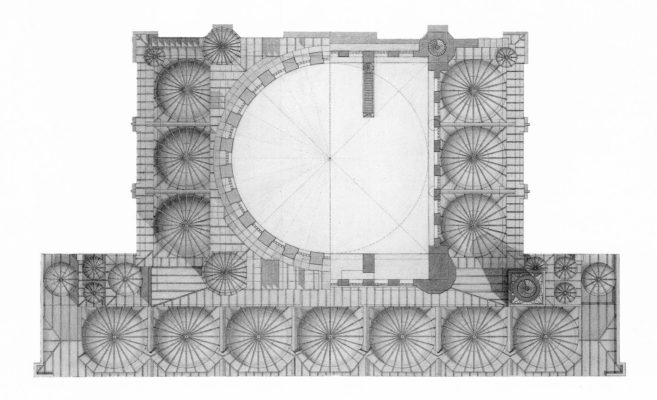

THE MIHRIMAH SULTAN CAMII.
SECTIONAL DIAGRAM (TOP) OF THE LEFT
HALF OF THE DOME AND THE RIGHT HALF
OF THE STRUCTURAL FRAMEWORK,
SHOWING THE REST OF THE MOSQUE'S
ROOF. ABOVE: A SECTION ORIENTED
TOWARD THE *KIBLA* (THE WALL TOWARD
WHICH WORSHIPPERS FACE) WHICH, IN
THIS MOSQUE, IS ON THE BRIGHTEST
FAÇADE. OPPOSITE: AN OVERVIEW,
SHOWN SIMULTANEOUSLY WITH
A TRANSVERSAL SECTION.

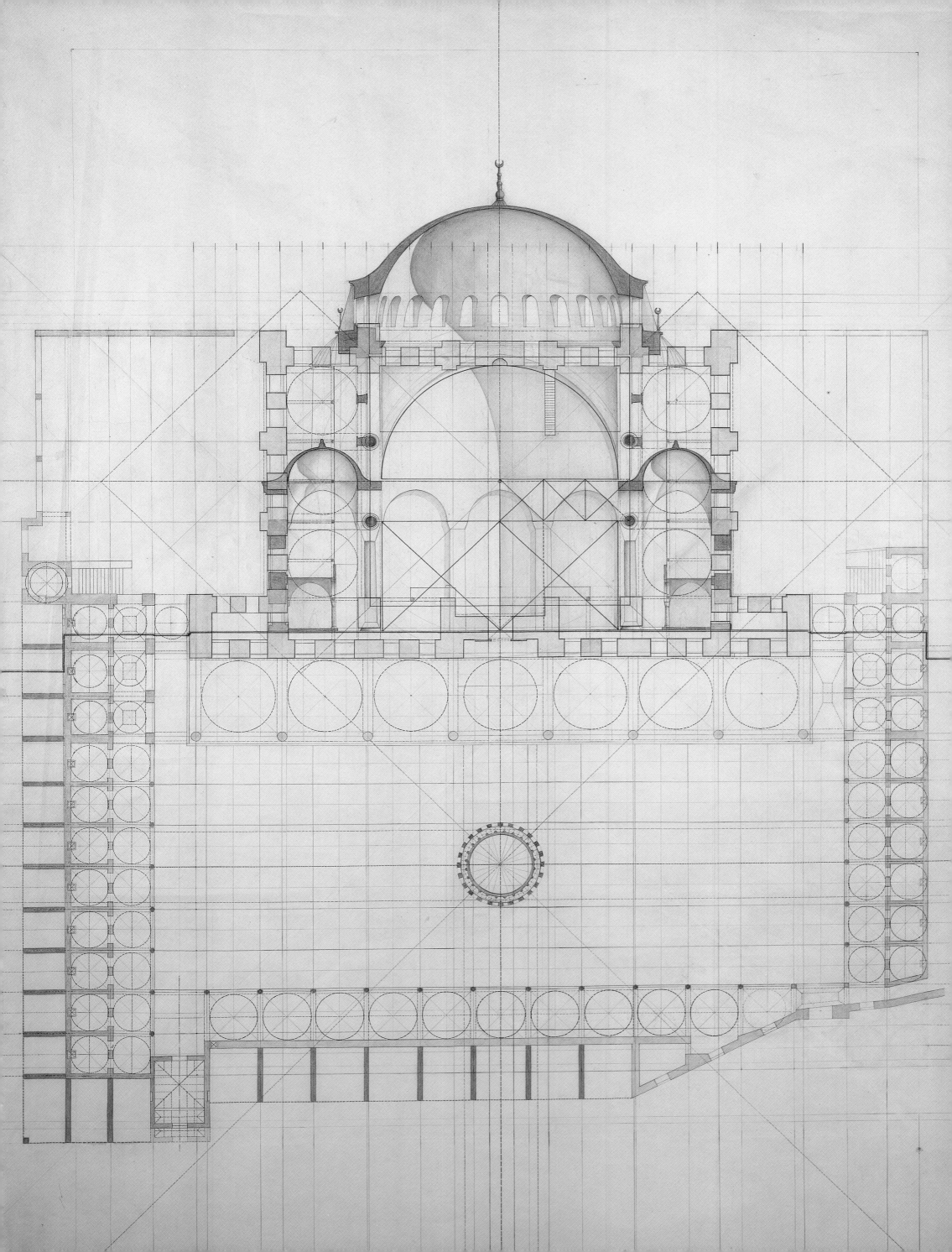

plan of the Istanbul *külliye* of Mehmet the Conquerer, the earliest such example, one sees that it is ordered in absolute symmetry – but its views are always partial. In the *külliye* of the Süleymaniye, the buildings housing the religious functions do not even form a pedestal for the mosque, given the nature of the site. In a *külliye*, the Koranic "dwell in Paradise wherever we please" becomes "enter the House of God from wherever we wish". The precinct entrances are small, numerous, widely dispersed and without hierarchy. The faithful arrive from and depart in all directions. This incessant movement intensifies at the hours of prayer. The gathering of the faithful is neither orderly nor processional. From the precinct entrances to the doors of the mosque itself there are oblique paved paths which to the Western eye appear to have been placed totally at random. The mosque does not dominate or impart order to the surrounding streets. Instead it dominates the whole city, and must be visible from afar, to guide the approaching traveller. The precinct isolates, but does not orient; it shields the sacred space of the mosque from the frenetic urban life surrounding it.

The *avlu* or enclosed forecourt serves as gathering place for those faithful who cannot find room inside the mosque on the occasions of special services. It is a kind of roofless prayer hall, with more than one *mihrab*, under the main portico. At the centre of the *avlu* stands the fountain for ablutions, its bulk partially obscuring the façade to those who come into the precinct by the entrance on the axis oriented toward Mecca. The other precinct entrances, like the lateral doors of the mosque itself, are not located along axes of symmetry; they are not designed according to laws of perspective. The *avlu* functions as an extension of the covered mosque, but it does not duplicate it. The fountain is placed squarely at the centre, and the main portico blocks the view of the façade. This is because, for those who pray in the *avlu,* a full view of the façade would underscore the fact that they are "outside" the mosque. Inside the mosque, if the space is to be absolute and unified, it follows that the prayer hall must not be gradually revealed to the onlooker but must appear suddenly, in its totality. This concept of vision, neither gradual nor perspective, has a significant precedent in the Ottoman way of handling three-dimensional imagery.

In a famous 1537 miniature by Matrakci Nasuh, court-painter during the reign of Süleyman the Magnificent, Istanbul is depicted within its walls and with all its contemporary monuments. There are, as yet, no Sinan mosques, but there are all the works dating back to the time of Mehmet the Conqueror. In this miniature, the buildings are drawn in elevation or in axonometric projection. In elevation, the viewer sees the building façades straight on, without indication of depth. In axonometric projection, two of the three axes are at right angles in the plane of the drawing; the third, which indicates depth, deviates to right or left at angles of less than 90°. For example, a flat square with lines extending from its corners at 45° angles and connected becomes a cube. In the Matrakci image this technique clarifies the relative positions of the objects shown: Istanbul seems as if painted, dimensionless, on a wall, while several buildings seem to be on the verge of tumbling out of the picture. Many miniatures preserved at the Topkapí Sarayí employ these methods of representation.

We do not know what techniques of representation Sinan used in his projects. But it is unlikely that they would have differed much from those just described. Strictly speaking, it would not have been necessary to use axonometric projection in Sinan's time. Then, wooden models were used that could represent a mosque three-dimensionally. But it is understandable that such a system of projection would appeal to the Ottoman culture – more for reasons of spiritual predisposition than for practicality. Axonometric projection freezes an object in its totality. It is a type of representation far less earthbound than perspective. To see things as they are seen with Western eyes presupposes a realistic, almost materialistic outlook – one thoroughly out of keeping with the teleological vision of the Islamic world. The axonometric projection, when seen from below, propels an object into space, removing it from the force of gravity, detaching it from the image in which it lies and leading it away from its earthly dimensions. The same method was followed in this book in illustrating the mosques. The tools used are the simplest – plane, section, axonometric section – providing the simultaneous projection of several views.

The study of Sinan's mosques is still in its early stages. Sinan was not fortunate enough to have a Giorgio Vasari to write an account of his life and works – there were only the poets, who unwittingly relegated the architect to the realm of legend. Until historians overcome the difficulties posed by language and calligraphy, and can fully explore the achives of the Topkapí Sarayí, we must try to perceive Sinan's genius through the patient, attentive observation of the buildings he left behind.

A LONGITUDINAL SECTION OF THE SELIMIYE (FOLLOWING PAGES). THE OCTAGONAL PRISM THAT CARRIES THE DOME IS INSCRIBED IN A SQUARE WHICH RISES TO THE TOP OF THE DOME'S FORTY WINDOWS. CONVERSELY, THE CIRCLE INSCRIBED IN THE DOME TOUCHES THE CORNICE FROM THE TOP OF THE GALLERIES. THE TRANSITION FROM THE SQUARE TO THE OCTAGON IS MADE BY STALACTITES, WHICH FORM PSEUDO-CAPITALS.

EDITIONS DIDIER MILLET
WISH TO THANK THE FOLLOWING FOR
THEIR INVALUABLE CONTRIBUTIONS
TO THIS BOOK:
PROFESSOR STÉPHANE YÉRASIMOS
LOUISE BRODY
CORINNE HEWLETT
ELI GOTTLIEB, JOHN TUTTLE AND
SHEILA MOONEY
ANNE NESTEROFF